JESUS UNPLUGGED

D0807497

JESUS UNPLUGGED

DAVE BURKE

Centre for
Faith and Spirituality
Loughborough University

Inter-Varsity Press

INTER-VARSITY PRESS
38 De Montfort Street, Leicester LE1 7GP, England
© Dave Burke

First published 2000

British Library Cataloguing in Publication Data
A catalogue record for this book is available from the British Library.

ISBN 0–85111–253–6

Set in Garamond
Typeset in Great Britain
Printed and bound in Great Britain by Cox & Wyman Ltd, Reading

Inter-Varsity Press is the book-publishing division of the Universities and Colleges Christian Fellowship (formerly the Inter-Varsity Fellowship), a student movement linking Christian Unions in universities and colleges throughout the United Kingdom, and a member movement of the International Fellowship of Evangelical Students. For more information about local and national activities write to UCCF, 38 De Montfort Street, Leicester LE1 7GP.

CONTENTS

PART THREE: Jerusalem

Maps

Tables and charts

Foreword

The last fifty years have seen Jesus of Nazareth take on many weird and wonderful personae, but none as wonderful as the real down-to-earth Jesus of the Bible. The Jesus of old conjures up images of blokes in dresses, strange-smelling smoke and holy water ('What's that all about?'), and, at the other extreme, people jabbering all over the place and speaking in funny languages, constantly grinning and clapping out of time. These are the images of the church. These are the images of Jesus.

Jesus Unplugged whips off the entire unnecessary mystique, corrects the folk stories, and invites Jesus into your living-room. He is allowed to let his hair down and tell the story the way it really is. Dave Burke manages to write a thoughtful, yet easy-to-read, account of the life of Jesus; his style is equally welcoming to Christians and those who are just looking.

Rarely does a book cut across so many boundaries in explaining the person and works of Jesus, but *Jesus Unplugged* manages to do just that without being heavy-going. The real Jesus springs to life with insight into the political and social atmosphere of the moment. This helps us to parallel the moral and spiritual condition of then and now, truly putting Jesus in the correct context.

When I began to investigate Jesus and the Christian religion, I was given books to read that were in the language of the 1970s. Every statement was followed by out-of-date words like 'fab' or 'groovy'! My utmost respect therefore goes out to Dave Burke for speaking in a relevant yet universal language that won't go out of fashion. Dave uses up-to-date stories from his life and other people's, but doesn't dress Jesus up in something he wouldn't be comfortable in. *Jesus Unplugged* stays true to the age-old message of the greatest figure in human history.

Read it, then give it away!

Cameron Dante

Acknowledgments

I want to record my gratitude to those who helped me with this project: first of all to Colin Duriez and the staff of IVP. Thanks also to Jo Bramwell, Nigel Pollock and Simon Jones for carefully reading and commenting on the manuscript. I have taken up almost all their suggestions, though any remaining faults are all my own work.

Thanks to the leadership team of Bethany Christian Centre for allowing me time to write this. Special gratitude is due to Ann Lindsay and Margaret Lewis, of our volunteer team, who have helped enormously by pretending to be Rottweilers and making superb tea. Thanks, girls! Alex Morris helped too, with her super essay on the miracles of Jesus.

Finally, a big thank you to my wife, Cathie, the living embodiment of Proverbs 31:10–31.

This book is for Jonny and Emma
Building bridges is a godlike thing to do,
Linking islands, making one instead of two.
God, if he came here,
Would be an engineer
He came
And was.

John Laurence

Read this First!

For the last three months of the second millennium a small white statue of a man occupied a massive plinth in Trafalgar Square, the heart of Britain's capital city. It looked lost beside the immense lions of state that flank Nelson's Column. The other statues in the square are at least three times life size, looking proud and accomplished on their mighty pedestals. But this man was tiny and insignificant, naked but for a loincloth, his hands tied behind his back, a circlet of thorns twisted three times round his head. Surrounded by the symbolism of a powerful nation, the sculpture seemed about to be crushed, just as the Roman state had once crushed the man it represented – Jesus of Nazareth.

I saw Mark Wallinger's statue of Jesus for the first time on my way to the National Gallery in November 1999. All around the world, millions of people were gearing up to celebrate the two-thousandth anniversary of the man the Romans crucified. This book is about him.

13

Let me tell you where I am coming from. I am a Christian and I want you to understand who this Jesus is (that's right, *is*, not *was*). This book is an introduction to his life and to the world in which he lived. It is also an introduction to his teaching. I have written it for people who do not know very much about him and would like to know more. If you are not a Christian, or you don't believe anything much, this book is for you. As you find out about Jesus, certain questions are bound to pop into your mind, and I have tried to answer some of these as we go. If you are a Christian, the chances are that your knowledge of the person you are supposed to be following is surprisingly skimpy. You too are welcome aboard. I hope you enjoy the journey!

Jesus' first followers wanted to preserve their memories of his life and teaching. As a result, four comprehensive accounts were assembled: those of Matthew, Mark, Luke and John. These books became known as *Gospels*, and are now part of the bigger book we call the Bible. The theological establishment of the twenty-first century promotes the view that the Gospels are largely mythology. In this book I have taken a radically alternative position; I believe that the Gospels' account is *at the very least* an honest attempt to describe what really happened, and I am asking you to be open to this possibility. (Actually, I believe they are more than this – that they are inspired by God himself – but I am not asking you to go that far … yet!)

Throughout my retelling of Jesus' life I have scattered references to these four writers. You do not have to look these up, especially as I have reproduced the important quotations verbatim in the text. Actual quotations from the Bible are in italics, *'like this'*. When you see a 'quotation' that is not italicized, it is my own paraphrase or summary of what was said.

When John wrote his great Gospel, he took a moment to explain his simple, overriding aim: '*that you may believe that Jesus is the Christ, the Son of God, and that by believing you may have life in his name*' (John 20:31). I have written this book with the same aim in mind.

The key events of Jesus' life in sequence

Winter 5/4 BC   Jesus is born in Bethlehem

4 BC   Herod the Great dies

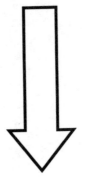

- Jesus family are
  refugees in Egypt

- They return to live in
  Nazareth

AD 29   John the Baptist begins his
                       ministry

Summer/autumn
AD 29   Jesus begins teaching and healing
                       in Galilee; he is in his thirties
                       according to Luke

                       John the Baptist is executed and
                       Jesus intensifies his activities
                       The disciples recognize Jesus as
                       the Messiah

                       The transfiguration

April AD 33   Jesus enters Jerusalem to
                       celebrate Passover with his
                       disciples

Jesus is crucified outside
Jerusalem

Resurrection appearances begin
soon after

May AD 33

After forty days of appearances
Jesus ascends to the Father

May AD 33 The apostles receive
the Holy Spirit and begin to
proclaim the resurrection

Based on H. W. Hoehner, 'Chronology', *Dictionary of Jesus and the Gospels* (IVP, 1992), p. 118.

PART ONE
Beginnings and sources

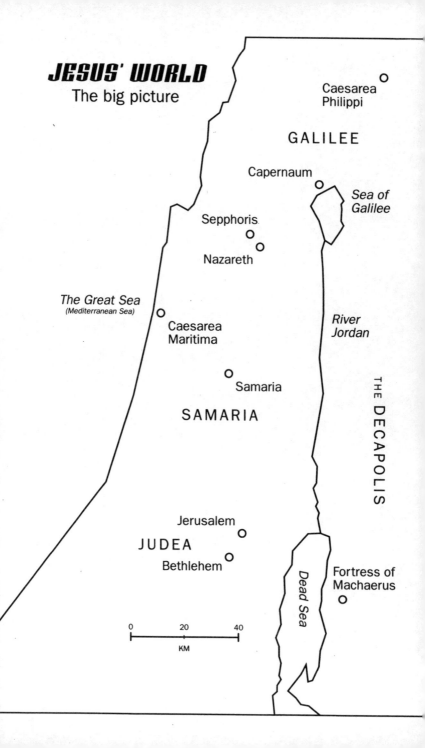

I

'Away with the Fairies?'

Picture the scene at the birth of Jesus. Jolly shepherds stand around a neat little crib in a pristine stable. Just outside are three kings, perched on camels. In an indigo sky, a bright star shines down on Mary and Joseph. Their little boy, nicely wrapped, lies in a feeding-trough. Doe-eyed cattle huddle up to the manger. 'All is calm, all is bright.'

To begin with, the story of the first Christmas looks like a myth. The Gospels say that a virgin conceived and gave birth to a child, whose arrival was predicted by angelic visitors and welcomed by a heavenly choir. Add this to a clean and cosy stable complete with supernova and a light dusting of snow, and you have the stuff of fairytales. It is tempting to think that Mark and John, who do not mention the birth of Jesus, took the easy way out. When I was a teenage atheist, I was tempted to sing, 'Away with the fairies! No crib for a bed, the little Lord Jesus lays down his sweet head.'

Actually, our beloved Christmas-card image, though

charming, is inaccurate. The stable was probably not a cave or a cattle-shed, but the part of a flat-roofed house where a family kept its cattle. It was often used for guests. It was also lined with years of built-up grime, like any farm building. The shepherds probably got there fairly quickly. These were local hill farmers and not popular with settled valley folk. The guys on the camels probably arrived a year or even two years later – and not on camels! The Christmas-card picture is a composite of all the events described by Matthew and Luke as interpreted by the Christmas industry over the centuries, rather than a representation of what actually happened.

In contrast, Matthew's and Luke's accounts of the birth of Jesus are realistically earthy. So that you can see what I mean, we are going to take a look at the least likely and believable members of the castlist: those exotic kings from the East. But first we need to think about a biological impossibility.

Virgin birth: who is Matthew trying to fool?

Seven hundred years before the birth of Jesus, a prophet called Isaiah had written of a virgin becoming pregnant and giving birth to a child. The name he gave the baby was 'Immanuel', which meant '*God is with us*' (Isaiah 7:14). This phenomenon and the special name were, according to the prophecy, a sign that God was about to move in and rescue his people.

Matthew applied the promise to Jesus, claiming that when Mary became pregnant she was a virgin. But that's not how Joseph, her fiancé, saw it. He knew he was not the father, and came to a more down-to-earth conclusion. The wedding was about to be called off when he had a dream. An angelic being spoke to him, saying that Mary's pregnancy was indeed the fulfilment of the prophecy, and that this virgin birth was the sign Isaiah had foreseen all those years ago. The incident was designed to underline the supernatural origin of Mary's child.

This cocktail of prophecy and virgin birth, with an angelic visitor thrown in for good measure, is not one that people in the modern world will easily swallow. Some Christians have tried to strip these stories out of the Gospels in an attempt to identify the 'real Jesus' underneath layers of myth. At its best, this search for the historical Jesus was aimed at helping modern people towards an authentic Christian faith. It sounds like an easy job, but it turned out to be impossible. The miracles are so deeply woven into the Gospel story that, if you strip them out, all you have left is a nice man who told nice stories. This has left the critics with a big problem. How could someone like this start the Jesus movement? They have struggled to answer that question convincingly.

The supernatural elements of Jesus' life are difficult to dismiss. If you are going to understand him at all, you must at least be open to the possibility that supernatural events can occasionally happen. Don't let Matthew's intoxicating brew put you off before you have heard the rest of the story, because from now on the plot-line is dominated by the claim that something new and dramatic was happening to bring human beings into a relationship with the supernatural God. Everything Jesus went on to do showed what happens when the power of this God becomes active in people's lives. If we start out by insisting that miracles cannot happen, we will not get far with Jesus. It isn't fair either; we need to approach the matter with an open mind.

And anyway, what is so impossible about a virgin birth? A human embryology lab has the technical ability to impregnate a virgin, so why can't God do this? The Gospels introduce us to the fact that God will sometimes do something completely off the wall to make a point. With Jesus, the point is that, though he is every inch human, there is a supernatural dimension to him that we must understand as well.

More about the miraculous later; but for now, what about those strange kings?

Seekers and dreamers

The actual words the Bible uses are important here. These men were not kings at all. Matthew called them *Magi*. An early Greek historian (Herodotus, 485–425 BC) described them as a tribe of Persians who followed the teachings of Zoroaster. Almost five hundred years later, Magi were still on the scene. They were interested in the occult and astrology, and occasionally dabbled in magic (the ancient word 'Magi' lies behind our word 'magician'). For the most part they were honest seekers after truth. Some, though, were shysters, like the Magus called Simon, who once tried to buy sole distribution rights for the Holy Spirit from one of the first Christian leaders (the story is in Acts 8:9–25).

Matthew's visitors, then, belonged to a sect that actually existed. But what made them take such a journey?

Six centuries before the birth of Jesus, their native country (probably Persia) had been home to thousands of exiled Jews. Ancient Jewish writings would have been in circulation among learned Persians. Their reading of these must have led them to the conclusion that a great king would be born one day in Judea, and that his birth would be signalled by a bright and unusual star.

They knew their way around the night sky, and the

sighting of a strange new star prompted their journey to Jerusalem, the capital of Judea and the origin of the ancient prophecy. A picture emerges of a people who mixed astrology with magic, and who would happily throw in a little Old Testament because it sounded intriguing. Just as modern scrap merchants collect old junk for recycling, they loved collecting and mixing ideas that made sense of the world, trying to find the real purpose behind everything. The Magi were seekers and dreamers, and risked the long journey to Jerusalem on the strength of a few verses of the Old Testament and an unusual celestial object. Were they completely insane? Maybe, but they were not the first 'alternative people' to find out that they were on to something, and they won't be the last.

Reporting the arrival of the Magi was Matthew's way of giving us a hint that the life of Jesus was a pivotal event in human history. 'People all around the world are going to be affected by this story,' he seems to be saying. 'In fact, it has already happened: look at these strange characters!'

Nothing daunted, the Gospel writers put in another large clue to the uniqueness of the child born in Bethlehem. He was, they point out, a member of an ancient royal family that had fallen on hard times.

The importance of breeding

I grew up with the story that my father's granddad was an Irish landowner who had fallen out with his family, had been disinherited and had come to England. It was a romantic idea. I remember lying in bed as a child and wondering if I really was the long-lost Duke of Dingle, and if one day my estranged family would turn up and restore me to my rightful inheritance and status in society.

One day we found my grandfather's birth certificate. The truth turned out to be more moving than the myth, though it blew my chances of ever becoming a duke. The fragile, old piece of paper confirmed that my great-grandmother was an immigrant from Ireland. It also told us that she couldn't write, for she had 'signed' the document with a cross. But great-grandfather was missing altogether, and the registrar had written 'Unknown' in the place where his name should have been. So my grandfather had been the illegitimate son of a poor Irish immigrant who couldn't name the father. It is there that any attempt to trace my genealogy further back comes to a halt.

I imagine that the real Duke of Dingle, if there is one, has a much better knowledge of his ancestry. Generally speaking, the more important members of society can trace their line back further than others. It was exactly the same in the Roman world when the four Gospels were being written. However rich and powerful, the Duke of Dingle has nothing on Jesus! At least, that's what Matthew and Luke want us to believe.

If you look at the first page of the New Testament, you will see that Matthew's Gospel begins with a long genealogy, tracing Jesus' ancestry way back through David, Israel's first king, to Abraham, the father of the Hebrew people (Matthew 1:1–17). Luke does the same thing slightly differently, taking Jesus' family tree all the way back to the first human beings mentioned in the Bible, Adam and Eve (Luke 3:23–38). These name-lists are a way of saying: 'Jesus is very significant indeed, far more important than anyone you have ever heard of.' The New Testament begins, then, with a massive claim about Jesus' status.

Of course, you could take the cynical view that

Matthew and Luke made all this ancestry up. The story of the Magi and these lists of glorious names were invented to pump up Jesus' importance. It is as though Jesus' first spin-doctors had hit on a way of exaggerating the status of their personal guru. This conclusion would make sense if it were not for one important fact: Jesus *has* turned out to be as significant as Matthew and Luke thought. The New Testament opens with a family tree that is really a fanfare to the greatness of Jesus, and it was written at a time when few could imagine what influence he would have. Now, if the sceptics are right, that was some accident!

Patterns in history?

His world is so far away from ours, and so long ago, that it is easy to forget how similar to ours it was in so many ways. Ordinary people lived their lives while the great events of history flowed around them. Battles were fought in distant countries, and few knew why or even cared. Paranoid officials signed papers that sent soldiers to slaughter innocent children. Political turmoil made law-abiding people into homeless refugees. In the midst of it all, some were caught up against their will in terrifying events, and others dropped out of society and launched out on weird adventures.

Sceptics like to see all this as an endless sequence of chance events in which the lucky prosper and the luckless suffer. But Matthew, like the other Gospel writers, sees a pattern in the chaos. Just as the Gulf Stream flows regardless of the chaotic movements of the Atlantic Ocean, so there is a Gulf Stream in the chaos of history. Matthew traces its flow in the genealogy in his first chapter, though the tragic, triumphant and titanic saga of the people of Israel. History is order masquerading as chaos, and the Jewish people are the current that makes sense of it. The flow leads directly to Jesus.

Looking for a king

The Magi arrived in Jerusalem looking for a king, and the natural place to go was the palace. This was of great interest to the reigning king, Herod the Great (37–4 BC). This king's paranoid brutality was legendary in the Roman world; he had murdered several of his own sons to secure his hold on power. When your people hate you as much as the Jews hated Herod, you can't afford to take any chances with prophecies, stars and children born to be king. The Old Testament experts among his aides were able to locate the promised king's birthplace using another of the Bible's ancient prophecies (Matthew 2:5–6). Thus they sent the Magi to Bethlehem.

Herod took these events very seriously. If they did find a child, it could have big consequences. With cold determination, he moved to neutralize the threat. Soldiers were quietly dispatched to seal off the town, with instructions to destroy any infant matching the travellers' description. A generous age limit of two years was specified. When the Persians left Bethlehem, the slaughter began.

Matthew's Gospel sets the story of the birth of Jesus not in mythology but in history. The Magi and their interest in the stars are matters of record – as is the exile of the Jewish people that would have left Old Testament scrolls circulating in Persian libraries. Then there is the brutal Herod, who did not shrink from ordering the execution of all the male toddlers in Bethlehem so that he could be sure he killed the right one. Matthew's description of the visit of the Magi is not so remote from reality as we might think. It is quite plausible.

Now, go back to the Christmas card and a more authentic picture of the scene. It is winter around 5 or 4 BC. There may have been a little snow. A man and his young wife are squeezed into the side-room of a little flat-roofed house. They share it with the owner's animals. It is a filthy place to have a baby. Mary and Joseph must deliver the child themselves. It is their first time, and they are frightened. Hill farmers arrive, but the locals don't want them there because they are regarded as thieves. They have lice, and their manners are rough. The room is crowded and squalid, and it would be cold if the animals didn't take the chill off the air. Mary and Joseph are dirt poor; all they have is what they had been able to carry, and there is almost no money. They settle briefly in Bethlehem, and after a year or so a group of travellers arrive, speaking an incomprehensible language, yet making it clear that they want to see the child. They leave expensive gifts and hurry away. Six miles away, in Jerusalem, a malevolent ruler ponders how to extinguish this new life.

The family would need those expensive gifts to finance a rapid flight into exile.

2
How can we know anything about Jesus?

You need two eyes to give you depth of vision. Right now, each of your eyes is sending a picture of the outside world to your brain. Each picture is slightly different. As you read this, the little differences between the signals from each eye are being compared by your brain and, bingo! You can see in 3-D! The value of two slightly different points of view is incalculable; having two eyes makes it much less likely that you will bump into a lamp-post, and gives you the 3-D picture you need to drive a car.

The Gospels give us more than two perspectives; they give us a four-sided portrait of Jesus. The first three are often called the *Synoptic* Gospels: that is, Matthew, Mark and Luke. 'Synoptic' is from a Greek word that means 'viewed together'. Imagine a Formula One Grand Prix. There are three people in the commentators' box, broadcasting their accounts of the race on three separate TV networks. They all say roughly the same thing, but each commentary is slightly different. The Synoptic

Gospels are like this. Matthew, Mark and Luke report Jesus' life from a similar vantage-point, as though they had been in the same grandstand. Just as with your eyes, the separate signals give a richer picture than you would get with only one.

The fourth Gospel is John, and it is as different from the others as chalk is from cheese. It is as though John had not been in the grandstand at all, but had spent the entire race in the pits interviewing the driver and mechanics. The result is a gospel that concentrates on a small number of events in Jesus' life, but with more analysis of what those events mean, and with more reportage of what Jesus himself said.

Of course, as soon as two people began to record Jesus' life there was the possibility of some conflict between the accounts they created. For the most part, the differences give us a fuller understanding of the events. Other differences pose more of a problem: for example, each Gospel records the resurrection in a rather different way. But this is not to say that the Gospels cannot be trusted as a source of reliable information about the life of Jesus. In fact, I want to try to show that they *can* be trusted.

Let's begin by imagining that they don't even exist.

Imagine there are no Gospels ...

Plenty of people were writing books in the first century AD. Several of these mention Jesus and his early followers. If we were to put together all the information available from these sources, we would know the following:

A man from Nazareth called Jesus lived in Galilee and in Judea when Pontius Pilate was the governor of that province. He had a brother called James. He became known as a great miracle-worker and teacher, and thousands of people were drawn to follow him. Some of them were Jews, though many were Gentiles. His miracles were inexplicable to both sympathetic and hostile observers. Some said that God was at work; others insisted that Jesus was a sorcerer. Pilate had him executed by crucifixion. His followers claimed that three days later he had risen from the dead, and many were prepared to die for this belief. The earliest communities of his followers worshipped him as a god. Within ten years of the crucifixion, people were being buried in Judea with inscriptions in their graves expressing the belief that they too would rise from the dead just like Jesus. Within twenty or thirty years, there were large numbers of Christians in Rome, the centre of the empire.

That summary was compiled from the writings of three people who lived in the first or second century, plus some extra detail from archaeological finds.

The first writer is *Josephus* (AD 37–101), a pro-Roman Jewish historian who wrote a history of the Jews. There is some suspicion that early Christians tinkered with manuscripts of his books, and it is quite possible (though not certain) that some over-zealous Christian scribes did insert a line or two into his work. I have not used the disputed lines of Josephus in the above summary.

The second source is *Tacitus* (AD 55–117), a Roman political commentator and historian who hated Christians ('a most mischievous superstition', he said). He explains why the Emperor Nero was persecuting the Christians in Rome.

The third writer is *Pliny the Younger* (AD 61–113), a

rather indecisive Roman governor in what is now Turkey, who outlined the practices of early Christian churches in his province. He didn't like the Christians either; 'a degenerate sort of cult, carried to extravagant lengths', he wrote. Two Christian women were tortured to help him reach that conclusion.

Lastly, some small archaeological finds mentioning the name of Jesus have contributed to the above picture.

Most people are surprised to learn that so much can be known about Jesus from books written by pagans and anti-Christian writers! All this is evidence that Jesus really lived, and that he made quite an impact on the Roman empire. The main elements of his life are corroborated from these non-Christian sources, and some of the beliefs and practices of the most primitive Christian believers are also revealed.

This is useful, but we can glean only so much from these sources of information. To discover more we need to assess the accuracy of the accounts of Jesus' life written by his followers.

Memory and poetry

In the first century, part of a rabbi's job was to teach his pupils to remember his teachings accurately. Jesus did the same, using traditional methods proven by the rabbis through the centuries; his words were couched in semi-poetic form, and even his stories had a certain rhythm to them and were easy to remember. As children, Jesus' disciples will have learned to memorize. It was an essential life-skill in their society; anyone who could not make the grade in it would simply not succeed.

Yet the cultures of Galilee and Judea were literate. A significant number of people could read and write, and written editions of the teachings of important rabbis were treasured. Most people have heard of the Dead Sea Scrolls, a huge cache of written material hidden in caves by a semi-monastic Jewish community around the time of Christ. Most of the documents are pre-Christian and testify to the period's abundance of written documents, to its writing skills and to a passion for collecting this kind of material.

Wherever Jesus went, he moved in literate circles and affected them deeply. It is impossible to imagine that people like this did not write down what they had experienced at the time or soon after. This combination of memorized and written materials, circulating among the first Christians, would have formed the first sources for those who began to feel the need to write down a fuller life of Jesus for future generations. Luke tells us that he has this kind of material in front of him as he writes his full and orderly arrangement of the life of Jesus. He had more than a few fragments; as it turns out, he had quite a library.

The scroll detectives

Luke's Gospel is especially important to me. After my first year at university, I was enjoying a climbing holiday in the French Alps when my friend and I decided to take a day away from the mountains. We drove to Geneva and spent the day admiring the city and looking at stuff we couldn't afford to buy in the shop windows. Towards the end of the afternoon we returned to our car. Under the windscreen wiper was a plastic bag with some papers inside. My heart sank. It looked as though we had been given a parking ticket.

It was not a parking ticket. Someone had carefully

wrapped a small English edition of Luke's Gospel in the plastic bag and left it there for us to find. I looked at it dubiously. I was not religious, and not very interested in the Bible; yet it was small and light, ideal for carrying with me in the mountains. I shoved it in my pocket and carried it with me for the rest of the summer. By September I was hooked, and I had to find out more about Jesus. As it turned out, Luke's Gospel was a great place to start.

He begins his biography of Jesus with a candid statement of its purpose:

> *Many have undertaken to draw up an account of the things that have been fulfilled among us, just as they were handed down to us by those who from the first were eye-witnesses and servants of the word. Therefore, since I myself have carefully investigated everything from the beginning, it seemed good also to me to write an orderly account for you, most excellent Theophilus, so that you may know the certainty of the things you have been taught* (Luke 1:1–4).

I was struck by the honesty of this opening. From his prologue we learn that Luke was not himself an eye-witness of the life of Jesus, though he had available to him material written by people who had seen what had happened. He also tells us that he has done his own research, carefully establishing the facts and intending to put it all down in an orderly or structured manner.

When I first read this statement, I wondered which writings Luke had in front of him as he set out to write his own account of the life of Jesus. Scholars have been researching this question for years, and their detective work has helped me to get some answers to this question. The next couple of pages may seem a bit technical, but in the end you will have an idea of how Luke probably got his information. What you are about to read is summarized in the diagram 'Where did Luke and Matthew get their information?'

I discovered that Luke almost certainly had the Gospel of Mark in his library, because about 90% of Mark's work is found in Luke. Mark does not tell us anything at all about the birth and childhood of Jesus and says tantalizingly little about the resurrection. Clearly, Luke felt that there were gaps to be filled, and he wanted to organize his material more logically.

Almost all researchers think Mark was the first Synoptic Gospel to be written. An early Christian writer called Papias, who lived in Rome around AD 140, said that Mark's Gospel was a record of the memories of the apostle Peter, and that, though it was an accurate account, it was not an orderly one. Another Roman Christian fondly remembered Mark by his nickname, 'Stumpy Fingers'! The memory that Mark was 'Peter's disciple and interpreter' was strong. Mark was concerned to record what Peter taught, and if Peter didn't teach it, Mark didn't write it. His is the shortest and fastest-moving gospel, just the right size for the busy citizens of Rome to fit into their Filofaxes.

It is clear that Luke depended on Mark's Gospel a great deal. But where did he get the rest of his information from? Once more the text detectives think they know the answer. Both Matthew and Luke record similar material that cannot be found in Mark, and it looks as though they have a document or documents that they are both copying from. The detectives call this source 'Q'; like the inventor of James Bond's gadgets. Luke, then, had an early version of Mark, and a collection of smaller documents that gave him the extra material he needed to supplement Mark's story. Look again at Luke's introduction: he tells us that 'many' had written about Jesus. So it seems likely that Luke and Matthew had quite a collection of written sources.

Luke had something else, too. He had discovered from a written source, or by speaking to Jesus' family, some of the more intimate details of Jesus' birth that Matthew couldn't have known about. Matthew, by the same token, had access to some material that Luke was probably unaware of. The detectives call these sources 'L' and 'M'.

This sounds more and more like a spy story as we go on. Congratulations! You have just made it through the most complicated part of the book!

This reconstruction of the development of the three Synoptic Gospels is not proven, though it is the most widely accepted among New Testament researchers. Even if you forget the details, one thing is worth remembering: Luke and his colleagues had a number of written accounts of the life of Jesus, and these must have been around soon after Jesus' death and resurrection.

Luke's Gospel is the longest, written in beautiful Greek and displaying a passion for accuracy. He was not content to tell us that John the Baptist preached in the wilderness; he felt compelled to say exactly when he began:

In the fifteenth year of the reign of Tiberius Caesar – when Pontius Pilate was governor of Judea, Herod tetrarch of Galilee, his brother Philip tetrarch of Iturea and Traconitis, and Lysanias tetrarch of Abilene – during the high priesthood of Annas and Caiaphas, the word of God came to John son of Zechariah in the desert. He went into all the country around the Jordan, preaching a baptism of repentance for the forgiveness of sins (Luke 3:1–3).

WHERE DID LUKE AND MATTHEW GET THEIR INFORMATION?

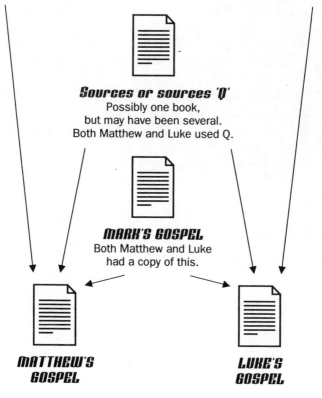

Sources 'M'
One or more books.
Only Matthew had these.

Sources 'L'
One or more books.
Only Luke had these.

Sources or sources 'Q'
Possibly one book,
but may have been several.
Both Matthew and Luke used Q.

MARK'S GOSPEL
Both Matthew and Luke
had a copy of this.

MATTHEW'S GOSPEL

LUKE'S GOSPEL

The striking thing about this passage is that Luke gets even the titles of the dignitaries exactly right. King Herod the Great's sons Herod Antipas and Philip are not kings or governors but *tetrarchs*. Now, I have just had to check my facts for the last sentence, because I couldn't remember whether Herod was their father or uncle. It was easy for me; I just popped into my local library. Luke didn't have that luxury. The only way he could get this sort of detail consistently right was by being close to the events, and by having good sources of information. This man was very well informed and very fussy.

It was this Gospel that changed my life. When I drove out to the French Alps with my friend I was a happy pagan, thoroughly enjoying my life and looking for nothing – well, not God, anyway! By the time we drove home I had gained an ambition. More than anything else I wanted to find out if Luke's story was true. I had to clarify a nagging doubt in the back of my mind. Had Luke just taken the story of an impressive country rabbi and made it into something much bigger, the story of the Son of God?

Gospel writers or spin-doctors?

We are familiar with the dark art of the spin-doctor, who takes the facts and puts the most favourable spin on them to further a political master's career. It is sometimes said that the writers of the Gospels were doing just this: reworking the life of Jesus so as to present an ordinary man as divine, and foisting their own theology on the world by putting their own words in his mouth.

Yet the first Christians worshipped Jesus as God before the Gospels were written. This is clear from early evidence, such as the information that Pliny's thugs tortured out of those two Christian women I mentioned earlier. Indeed, this was the reason so many of them faced such cruel persecution. As Roman megalomania grew, the empire's subjects were obliged to worship the emperor as divine. The Christians refused to do so, out of loyalty to Jesus, and they suffered horribly as a result. The Gospel writers didn't need to present Jesus as divine, since most Christians had already made their minds up on that issue.

In fact, if Luke and Co. were intending to put a favourable spin on the life of Jesus, they could have done a better job. They included information that has often been used to discredit him. As we have seen, Matthew's Gospel begins with a portrait of Jesus as royalty and presents him as the Son of God. But it finishes with his being crucified and saying, '*My God, my God, why have you forsaken me?*' (27:46) Now, if I were Matthew, I would have left that rather embarrassing low point out of my presentation. You will find many other details in the Gospels that an intelligent spin-doctor would have omitted, yet they are kept in for the world to read. There is real integrity at work here.

The essence of spin is to be simple, repetitive and easy to understand. The Gospels are the opposite, full of information that could easily be used against their central claim. They tell a story of great complexity, and seem keen to miss nothing out, even if it prejudices their case. If the Gospel writers strike some people as naïve, it is because of their simple commitment to the truth. They believed that they should tell the amazing story of Jesus just as it really was.

Let's return to that story.

PART TWO
Galilee

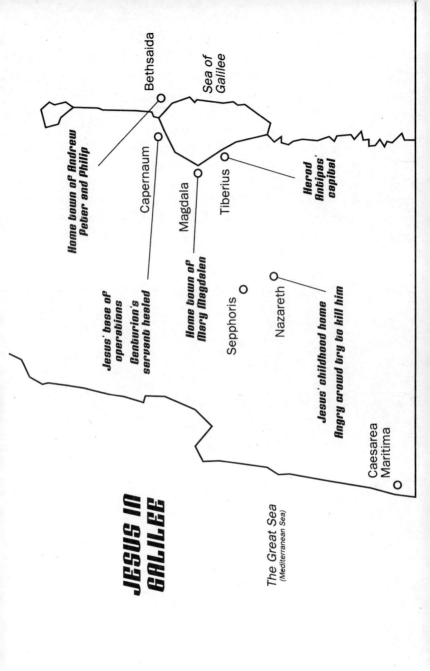

JESUS IN GALILEE

Bethsaida
Sea of Galilee

Home town of
Peter and Andrew
Philip

Capernaum

Magdala

Tiberius

Herod
Antipas'
capital

Jesus' base of
operations
Centurion's
servant healed

Home town of
Mary Magdalen

Sepphoris

Nazareth

Jesus' childhood home
Angry crowd try to kill him

Caesarea
Maritima

The Great Sea
(Mediterranean Sea)

3

Growing up in Galilee

If Herod's executioners had succeeded, we would never have heard of Jesus. In many ways his escape from Bethlehem was remarkable. Some historians estimate the population of the town at that time to be about a thousand people. This being the case, the likely number of boys under two years old would be around twenty. It must have been hard to get away from a community like this without being noticed and betrayed. According to Matthew, Joseph played a large part in evading the trouble.

Meet the family

Christians have tended to put Mary, the mother of Jesus, on a pedestal. But Joseph, his father, deserves more recognition than he gets. To begin with, when he discovered that his wife-to-be was pregnant, he drew the obvious conclusion. Yet, if he felt outraged, he didn't take it out on Mary. Instead, he decided to hush up the affair and quietly dissolve the betrothal arrangement. As we have seen, he was then reassured in a dream that Mary's was a supernatural pregnancy.

There is no doubt that, as far as Matthew was concerned, Joseph was a dreamer. Four times in Matthew's first two chapters, Joseph has dreams that inspire crucial decisions. He comes over as an ordinary man who had the knack of listening to God and the courage to act on what he heard. The result was a long trip to Egypt, way off to the south and west, to avoid death at the hands of Herod.

Though his guidance was unusual, the decision to go to Egypt had a hard-headed logic to it. A Jewish philosopher called Philo Judeus (20 BC–54 AD) was alive around this time. He tells us that there was a huge number of Jews living in Egypt; he put it at around a million, though this may be an exaggeration. According to Philo, they were concentrated in his home city of Alexandria. It was a natural place for refugees like Mary and Joseph to make for. Here they would find the things they most needed: people who spoke their language, as well as support and sympathy from other victims of Herod's brutality. Also, their co-religionists would be likely to give Joseph work.

Joseph was a carpenter, by the way. Much later, one of Jesus' critics would caustically dismiss him as *'the carpenter's son'* (Matthew 13:55). Jesus will have learned his father's trade. This did not mean he made a living assembling flat-pack furniture. Building gadgets made of wood involved many first-century engineering problems. A carpenter had to be skilful enough to solve any of them. A large part of Jesus' childhood would have been spent helping his father to make things, and he would have picked up a variety of skills as he went along.

The family's stay in Egypt lasted some years, and came to an end after another of Joseph's dreams. Herod the

Great had died, so they were able to return to Judea. They settled in the northern province of Galilee, wanting to live not too close to Jerusalem, the seat of power of Herod's son, Archelaus. Again, the dreams had a happy logic to them. Within two hours' walk of Nazareth was the new and growing city of Sepphoris, a major commercial centre where Joseph may well have found work to support his young and growing family. There is some speculation that Jesus spent a lot of time in this cosmopolitan city, and would therefore have had wider experience of the world's cultures than most Jewish boys.

In the synagogue, Jesus would learn about his nation's history and memorize chunks of the *Torah*, the ancient Scriptures of the Jewish people that now feature in what we call the Old Testament. Yet some of Jesus' adult expressions may have been picked up from Gentiles on the building sites of Sepphoris. For instance, 'hypocrite', one of his favourite words, was Greek, not Jewish, in origin. A *hypocritē* was an actor in the Greek theatre, someone who made a living pretending to be someone else. Jesus would one day turn this word against those whose religion was a piece of sanctimonious theatre.

Jesus was probably the eldest of a number of children. Matthew mentions the names of four of his brothers and an unspecified number of sisters (13:55–56). We know little of what happened to Jesus' siblings, though several of them would later become his followers. Most prominent among these was James, who seems to have become the leader of the first Christian community in Jerusalem.

We know little about the family that settled in to its new home in Nazareth after its travels in Egypt, and we have identified just about all the facts Matthew was interested in. Luke gives us a little more information: Jesus and John the Baptist were related (see Luke 1:36); and soon after Jesus' birth Mary and Joseph went to the temple in Jerusalem to offer the customary sacrifices on behalf of their firstborn (see Luke 2:22–24). The fact that they offered the cheapest possible sacrifice, two pigeons, indicates that Jesus' family was poor and had no money to spare.

The town of Nazareth was in Galilee, a region of low hills, about the size of Rhode Island or the Isle of Wight. Well watered and fertile, growing mainly olives and cereals, its eastern border was the Sea of Galilee (or Lake of Gennesaret), where a prosperous fishing industry was based. Josephus, the Jewish historian we met in the last chapter, wrote, 'The lake contains species of fish different in taste and appearance from those found elsewhere'. The fish were dried, and were sold as far away as Rome.

Galilee was not a rural backwater. Being crossed by several important roads, it had good communications with the rest of the empire, and boasted some large settlements. In Jesus' time it was wooded and productive, but in the centuries after the Roman occupation, Galilee declined. Today, the hills are covered by *maquis*, a dense and impenetrable scrub, the base vegetation of virtually the whole Mediterranean region. Most of the settlements Jesus knew and visited have disappeared.

Nearby, the towns of Capernaum and Bethsaida have been extensively excavated by archaeologists. This is where Jesus was based during the early period of his public work. The homes of people who would have known him personally have been uncovered. It was not a poor settlement, and the remains of houses in Capernaum and Bethsaida reveal that some of Jesus' earliest followers would have enjoyed a good standard of living.

Jesus goes missing

Luke, alone among the Gospel writers, gives us a detailed description of one incident in Jesus' childhood. During a family trip to Jerusalem, he went missing, and his parents spent several anxious days trying to find him. He was only twelve at the time, so it must have been traumatic for the rest of the family. Eventually, they discovered him in the temple, enthusiastically probing the teachers of the law with questions and carefully absorbing their answers (see Luke 2:41–52). The incident made a profound impression on Mary, who *'treasured all these things in her heart'*. Luke adds the comment: *'Jesus grew in wisdom and in stature, and in favour with God and men.'* The implication is that Jesus did not grow up as a remote and self-consciously religious child, but that people liked him, respected his opinions and found him a good person to have around. He was a part of ordinary people's lives and he seems to have enjoyed it.

This is a good moment to think about the differences between Matthew's Gospel and Luke's. Though they tell substantially the same story, it is puzzling that Luke never even hints at the dramatic escape into Egypt, and Matthew seems not to be aware of the exciting fact that Jesus once went missing in Jerusalem. An obvious explanation could be that each writer was genuinely unaware of the incidents he failed to record in his Gospel. But it seems more likely that each was carefully selecting and arranging his material and deliberately leaving out other information. Matthew possibly knew about Jesus going missing and decided not to use the story, but couldn't resist putting in the account of Jesus' family's return from Egypt, and highlighting it with a quotation from an old prophecy (Matthew 2:15). It was his way of dropping a hint that Jesus was going to be a bit like Moses, who had led God's people out of slavery in Egypt and taught them how God wanted them to live. (The story is told in the section below.)

It is important to know that each of the four Gospels was written to appeal to different sorts of readers; Matthew's Gospel is overwhelmingly Jewish in feel, and Luke's is a very Greek document. Both were written to persuade people to follow Jesus and to help the committed to keep their Christian faith alive. So each writer put in the material he thought would best do these things for his original readers.

Luke wanted his Greek readers to know about Jesus' astonishing wisdom as a child, because '*Greeks look for wisdom*' (1 Corinthians 1:22). Mark and John did not think their readers would be so interested in his childhood, and they wrote nothing about it. Matthew's Gospel was written for Jews. It sets out to show that everything their people had experienced throughout their history was a preparation for the coming of Jesus.

This brings us to the one fact we do know about the early formation of Jesus' ideas: he was Jewish.

Jesus' Jewish roots

When Mary and Joseph took Jesus to the temple in Jerusalem to be circumcised, they were observing rituals that had been part of the life of their community for many hundreds of years. So much of Jesus' teaching drew on this background that we must take a little time to understand it. The story of the nation of Israel formed a vital part of the psychological landscape of Jesus' first hearers.

The saga is told in the collection of books we now call the Old Testament. It begins with a nomadic trader called

Abraham, who lived in what we now call Iraq until he moved westwards to reside near the city of Hebron in the land of Canaan, in modern Israel. After his death, Abraham's extended family migrated to Egypt to escape a famine. They stayed for several generations. As time passed, these immigrants were branded as a potential threat and were held in slavery by Egyptian taskmasters.

Then an Israelite called Moses emerged as their leader and organized his people to make a successful bid for freedom. The story of this event, remembered today as the exodus, is brilliantly retold in Steven Spielberg's movie *Prince of Egypt*. In the course of a mass flight from slavery into the Sinai desert and freedom, Abraham's descendents became a recognizable nation with its own laws and judicial system. The five books of Moses (or the Torah, or the Law) were the main religious influence on the world Jesus grew up in. In our Bibles they are the books of Genesis, Exodus, Leviticus, Numbers and Deuteronomy.

Forty years later, Israel moved out of the desert and across the River Jordan to occupy the land of Canaan. Succeeding generations fought off the predatory peoples from round about, and the nation became a settled kingdom under David, son of Jesse. David built his capital on the site we now call the Temple Mount in Jerusalem. His reign, and that of his son, Solomon, are still regarded as Israel's finest hour.

This new kingdom prospered under Solomon, whose wealth and wisdom made him one of the most famous of the Israelite kings to this day, but whose inept handling of his affairs in later life would cause the fracture the kingdom after his death. In time, Solomon's successors would experience bitter hardship at the hands of some of the military bullies in the region. The Assyrians invaded the northern kingdom, Israel, and carried off its population to their own land as slaves. Some time later, the southern kingdom, Judah, was attacked by the Babylonians and many of its citizens were marched off into exile. The trauma of these experiences can scarcely be imagined.

The people taken into captivity in Babylon (now known as Jews) clung to their national identity with incredible tenacity. They were never absorbed into the culture of the Babylonians. When that great city fell to the invading Persians, they resisted the attractions of Persian culture too.

When the Persians permitted them to return to their own land, they were able to rebuild their national life and start again. But what they had after the exile bore no resemblance at all to the glory of Solomon's kingdom, and for the next few hundred years they were a client state, first of the Persians, and then of the Greek empire of Alexander the Great. By the time of Christ, Judah had become the Roman province of Judea, and their brutal king a mere *apparatchik* of the mighty Roman administration. This is the background to the history that Matthew is rehearsing in his long genealogy at the start of his gospel.

But the Jews believed they were more than a people with a common history; they were convinced they were a *chosen* people with a common history. The Old Testament is dominated by this thought. Abraham was chosen to be the father of a great nation (see Genesis 12:1–3). It was not by virtue of clever leadership and cunning that Israel escaped from Egypt; God acted on their behalf because he regarded them as his chosen people (see Exodus 4:22–23). Moses did not invent the laws of Israel; God gave them to the nation himself, so that they would stand apart from the other nations in their religious and legal practices. The terrible exile in Babylon was the result of failure to adhere to the laws they were given, the final reminder that their privileges as God's chosen people were accompanied by responsibilities to behave accordingly.

As the Babylonian exile became more and more inevitable, the people of Israel and Judah were confronted by men, and occasionally women, who tried by their preaching to pull the people of God back to obedience to the law and thereby to avert disaster. These people were called 'prophets'. Some of them, such as Jeremiah and Isaiah, are still well known today, even if they are not exactly household names. Their message may have been ignored by their own generation, but it became fundamental for the Jews who returned from exile. They had learned to obey the law of God even when surrounded by seductive Persian culture, and this helped them to resist the dilution of their religion by the Greeks and then the Romans. By the time Mary and Joseph went to buy those two pigeons to sacrifice in the temple in thanksgiving for Jesus' birth, the goals of the Jewish leadership were clear. They wanted to maintain religious and racial purity in the face of the vigorous mixing of cultures taking place in the melting-pot of the Roman empire, maintaining obedience to the law of Moses and the writings of God's prophets at all costs.

Growing up Jewish

As Jesus grew up he would slowly become aware of his Jewish heritage. Nazareth had a synagogue, the centre of teaching and worship he and his family attended every week. He heard the books that make up the Old Testament being read and explained by teachers accredited by the temple in Jerusalem. These words sank into his memory; he would often quote them verbatim in later life.

The interpretations of the teachers of the law affected him too. As an adult he would find himself in sharp conflict with these very people and the religious establishment of which they were part.

He learned of the history of Israel in the family celebrations required by the law. Most important of these was the Passover, a family drama re-enacted each year to remind everyone how God rescued the nation from slavery in Egypt. His adoptive father, Joseph, would preside at this. Every year, Jesus would watch his dad lift the bread up so that the family could see it, and hear him recite the traditional words: 'This is the bread of affliction, the poor bread which our fathers ate in the land of Egypt. Let all who are hungry come and eat. Let all who are in need share in the hope of the Passover.' The words and the pictures they evoked would burn themselves into Jesus' consciousness as he grew up.

Occasionally, the family would make the required pilgrimages to the great festivals held in Jersusalem. For a young boy from a rural community, this would have been an amazing experience. The crude temple hurriedly erected by the exiles returning from Babylon had been demolished and replaced by a breathtaking new structure that dominated the city's skyline. Added to this were the palace and fortress built by Herod the Great. Jews from all over the known world would converge on Jerusalem at the same time, babbling away in a dozen or so languages. These days were like holidays and church services rolled into one. Jesus would be playing with his friends one minute and face to face with the entrance to the sacred temple the next. Perhaps someone read to him the plaque, inscribed in Latin and Greek, recently dug out of the ruins of this temple and dating from Jesus' time: 'No non-Jew to proceed beyond the barrier and enclosure which surround the sacred place; any man who does so and is caught is himself responsible for his death, which is the consequence.'

It was in these very precincts that Jesus' frantic parents found him asking questions and listening to the teachers' answers. If you believe Luke's story (and I do; why couldn't Jesus be a child prodigy?), Jesus emerges as a youngster with an uncanny sense of his own uniqueness. *'Why were you searching for me?'* he asked. *'Didn't you know I had to be in my Father's house?'* (Luke 2:49).

Jesus was not the only member of his family who would grow up to question and criticize the *status quo*. We have already met his relative John. John's parents were from an ancient priestly clan. He too saw the hypocrisy that compromised the religious life of his nation. Before Jesus left his day job to teach and preach, John had achieved national prominence with his own ministry. He was an uncompromising radical who demanded that people repent and allow him to give them a ritual dip in the River Jordan, a symbolic wash that represented their change of life. The ritual gave him his nickname, 'the Baptist'. His style was confrontational and unbending. Not even the royal family was spared his uncompromising criticism. This was to get him into deep trouble.

4

Into the wild country

The wilderness to the north of the Dead Sea was not noted for its nightlife. So John the Baptist, up to his knees in muddy water and holding forth for all he was worth, was good entertainment, if you didn't mind the entrance fee: a weary walk in the desert heat to a remote river bend.

Some had made the trip because they could no longer face the daily grind of their hopeless lives. Others felt drawn by God to hear this strange prophet in the desert. Some were there for health reasons; secret agents were on the look-out for them and it would be bad for their health if the Romans ever found them. There they all were, listening to John in the cool morning by the river; mothers and children, grannies and freedom fighters, religious freaks and farm hands.

'Repent!' John's voice echoed down the valley, 'Repent, because the kingdom of heaven, bringing the judgment and wrath of Almighty God, is near.' His wild and uncompromising message was drawing to a climax. 'God's axe is already raised,' he shouted. 'The blade is about to fall and destroy you. So turn from your sins, change your behaviour, and show you are serious by letting me baptize you.'

He waded into the river until he was waist deep in the brown water. Just then, his eye caught the amused smile of a clergyman nudging his friend. 'Who warned *you* to flee from the wrath to come?' John asked menacingly. 'Repent, and show God that your lives have changed. Your religious qualifications mean nothing to him!'

As John scanned the audience, people began to come to the edge of the water. One by one they waded out to join him and quietly confessed their sins. Then he took them by the shoulders and pushed them under, each time repeating the same quiet incantation: 'Because you repent, I baptize you with water. But wait for the one who will baptize you with the Holy Spirit and with fire.'

While some of the people waded awkwardly towards John, few noticed a young man at the back of the crowd who began to push his way forward and take his place in the river with the others. John took the shoulders of each penitent, saying 'Confess your sins, and I will baptize you.' Then he would push the person under the water and, a moment or two later, help him or her back to the bank. When the young man's turn came, John began his incantation again: 'Confess your sins, and I will ...' But this time his voice trailed off. Face to face with the stranger, John smiled for the first time that day. He held out his hand. 'Jesus!' he exclaimed. 'What are you doing here? I should be baptized by you, not the other way round!'

A prophet like the old days

John the Baptist had become a one-man opposition party, delivering his harsh critique from the wilderness and inviting people to respond to God personally by receiving his baptism. John even merits a long section in Josephus' history of his people. In his day, John was headline news.

Yet it is clear from the Gospels that he was always going to be upstaged by Jesus and that his real job was to prepare the way for this even greater individual. John was the fulfilment of yet more ancient prophecy: *'This is he who was spoken of through the prophet Isaiah: "A voice of one calling in the desert, 'Prepare the way for the Lord, make straight paths for him'"'* (Matthew 3:3).

Whenever an eastern monarch rode out of his palace, he would have to pass through filthy streets crowded with the kind of people he really didn't want to mix with, or even see. So he would send outriders before him to clear the locals out of the way, move the garbage, and get people ready to greet their lord with suitably joyous and respectful cries. No doubt a little gentle persuasion was needed, especially if the big guy was unpopular. Though John was not announcing this kind of despotic king, nevertheless this was his job. He was to announce the imminent arrival of the Messiah, call people to prepare for him, and then let him take over when the time came. John was Jesus' outrider.

Is there such a thing as fulfilled prophecy?

Of course, it is always possible to dismiss Matthew's and Luke's belief that prophecy was being fulfilled, and to suggest that they have written up their stories to make it look as though these old predictions were coming true.

You don't need a degree in theology to make this kind of suggestion, though many academics have argued strenuously that this is exactly what the Gospel writers were up to. At the back of this view is a belief that no human being can ever predict events far in the future. So all claims that prophecy has been fulfilled must be fraudulent. Therefore, no matter what the Gospel writers say about John and Jesus fulfilling Old Testament prophecy, it cannot be true and they must be making it up.

Yet the Gospel writers do invite us to be open to this possibility. They are continually referring to ancient promises, dreams and pictures as being directly fulfilled in the events they themselves describe. At the heart of this practice lies a conviction that God is working to a plan, that parts of his strategy have been leaked over the centuries to the prophets of Israel, and that the plan is moving to a climax in the lives of John the Baptist and Jesus.

John, then, baptized his friend Jesus. Immediately, God's Spirit, in the symbolic form of a dove, fluttered up and landed on him as a disembodied supernatural voice affirmed: *'This is my Son, whom I love; with him I am well pleased'* (Matthew 3:17). This detail is very important. Jesus' amazing abilities were not magical, or advanced science, but (as he would insist throughout his life) the power of God working through him. At the end of his ministry he would tell his followers to wait until this same Holy Spirit descended on them, individually and corporately, before they attempted the job of taking his message around the world. The Christian movement that developed would, like Jesus, attribute its effectiveness and dynamic growth to the power of this Holy Spirit working through it. His twenty-first-century followers believe that it is the same today: the Spirit who came upon Jesus at his baptism empowers the Jesus movement even now.

An appointment with evil

Now that Jesus had been confirmed as God's Son, this would have been a good moment to make for Jerusalem. If he was part of a divine plan to change the world, where better to begin than the city at the heart of this plan? Surely now was the time for some stimulating debate with those influential scholars he had met as a twelve-year-old? But he did not go to the capital. Instead, he walked further into the wilderness, where he stayed for well over a month, going without food.

It was easy to get to the wild country from the centres of population in Galilee and Judea, but it was not so easy to survive there. Nevertheless, Jesus was not the only person in first-century Palestine to practise extreme fasting in this wild country. All kinds of spiritual 'hard-men' have done this sort of thing before and since. What made Jesus' wilderness experience unique was the encounter he had there with Satan.

The nature of evil

Some people are uneasy about the idea of a real, personal devil, and, although we speak of some people as evil, we tend to put this down to social and psychological factors rather than to an evil being who works through them. Joseph Stalin and Adolf Hitler come to mind. Six million Jews were murdered under Hitler and at least twenty million Russians under Stalin, and these are just the top two examples on the long league table of genocides in the last century. Were these men inspired by evil, or just responding to their upbringing and environment? Is there a person called Satan who inspires such acts?

Let's start by getting rid of the myth that only a few

individuals can be described as evil. In his book *Hitler's Willing Executioners*, Daniel Goldhagen demonstrated that tens of thousands of ordinary European citizens co-operated with the systematic killing of Jewish men, women and children. They didn't have to, but they did. Evil is not, it seems, located only in the hearts of a few bad guys. We are all susceptible to its influence. The likes of Stalin and Hitler seem more evil than others because they have the knack of bringing out the potential for evil in the rest of us and focusing it to achieve their own aims.

According to the writers of the Gospels, Satan is doing this on a worldwide scale. They do not attribute *all* our wrongdoing to him, but they do say that he lies behind the evil in the world. He is able to bring out our sinfulness and put it to work for himself, so that we are in some ways his slaves.

He first appears in the opening chapters of the Old Testament. Here he is encouraging the first human beings to disobey God. He succeeds, and in their disobedience the first humans develop a bias towards sinful behaviour. After this, Satan appears surprisingly infrequently, though readers of the Old Testament are reminded from time to time that he is there. Human beings can sin very effectively without him, it seems, though like a hidden puppet-master he pulls the strings from time to time. Our human 'devils', such as Hitler and Stalin, are only pale imitations of the real thing; the malevolence and cruelty of Satan can scarcely be imagined.

The puppet-master

In the New Testament we learn a lot more about Satan, and it becomes clear that he must in some way be defeated if human beings are to be liberated and the puppet strings cut.

Matthew, in his account of Jesus in the wilderness, calls Satan '*the tempter*' (4:3). His nature is to encourage the bias to sinfulness in us, to try to get us to cooperate with evil and to participate in evil activity. This does not have to be mass murder or hideous cruelty. Petty selfishness or spite will do nicely, as long as we make our own contribution to the moral mayhem on the world stage, or in our own little world. In the wild country, Satan met Jesus and tried to pull him into this whirlpool. His goal was to get Jesus to walk away from God's plan and to cooperate with evil, just as he had once put pressure on the first human beings to do the same.

It is difficult to know how we are meant to imagine the temptation of Jesus described in the Gospels. He is close to starvation, and the suggestion comes to him that he could use his power to make stones into bread. Did Satan come in human form and speak, or was all this going on inside Jesus' head?

Next, the devil takes Jesus to Jerusalem and perches on a high point on the temple. He suggests that Jesus may like to show how special he is by jumping off and letting an angel catch him. Did Satan and Jesus walk to the temple, or was Jesus 'beamed' there, *Star Trek* style? Or is this an out-of-body experience, while Jesus is still physically in the desert? We just don't know.

The final venue is a high mountain, from which Satan shows Jesus all the kingdoms of the world. You couldn't get a view like that even from the top of Everest. Was this a vision of some kind, rather than a trip to a real mountain? Whatever it was, Satan showed Jesus the view and offered him the earth, if only he would submit himself to the devil's rule and swim with the tide of evil.

It isn't hard, however, to work out what is going on. Satan was using his power to try to deflect Jesus from following God's purpose. In the desert he attempted to create self-interest, vanity and cowardice within Jesus, and to recruit him to serve his evil purposes. The result was failure. There was no evil in Jesus, no self-interest, no pride, no greed, no cowardice, nothing for Satan to get his teeth into. Jesus' response to each of his suggestions was a curt and apt quotation from the Torah. The pressure was off, and a half-starved and exhausted man found himself alone in the desert.

The first Christian writers put great emphasis on the fact that Jesus was without sin. His great friend, Peter, once applied to him a quotation from the Old Testament: *'He committed no sin, and no deceit was found in his mouth'* (1 Peter 2:22). This was not the last temptation of Jesus, and it was possibly not the first. The Gospel writers put the story at the beginning of Jesus' working life as a teacher as though to show that he had passed some kind of spiritual test, and was now ready for his life's work. But he held back, as if waiting for some unmistakable signal to begin his work in earnest. Before long that signal came. The uncompromising John the Baptist was in trouble. He was under arrest and imprisoned on the orders of Herod.

John's appointment with evil

As we saw in the last chapter, this was not the Herod who had had the children of Bethlehem killed when Jesus was a baby. Herod the Great had long since died, and his kingdom had been divided into three regions, each ruled by a 'tetrarch'. His son Herod Antipas was now tetrarch of Galilee, where John was now operating. Mark's Gospel tells us that this Herod had rid himself of his first wife so that he could marry the wife of his brother Philip. John the Baptist had confronted the tetrarch on the issue because he had broken Jewish law. Herod was prepared to listen to John, but his new wife, Herodias, nursed a grudge against him and wanted revenge.

The story is vividly confirmed by the Jewish writer, Josephus, who had an intimate knowledge of the affairs of his homeland. He tells us that John's criticism of Herod's marriage was not the only reason the tetrarch acted as he did. He had become suspicious that John's followers could turn into a revolutionary movement that would lead to insurrection. So Herod felt he had to move against John to safeguard his position and to keep his new wife happy. Having John arrested and put in prison killed two birds with one stone.

The forerunner's work was over, and Jesus now intensified his ministry, taking over where John had left off.

5
Giving up the day job

The synagogue in Nazareth was a simple, rectangular building with two rows of columns supporting the roof. There was a bench seat right round the wall, and a plain paved floor. A small raised area at one end had space for a lectern, where the scrolls were read aloud. The scrolls themselves, containing the Law and the Prophets, were in a box just behind. Outside Jerusalem there was no elaborate Jewish architecture. There were no pictures on the walls, or statues to worship. The Jews believed that God is invisible and that he ought to stay that way.

John's arrest now stimulated Jesus to step up his activities. As a respected member of his own synagogue in Nazareth, he was asked to read from the scrolls one Sabbath. He chose a passage in Isaiah, a prophecy about the coming of the Messiah:

The Spirit of the Lord is on me,
because he has anointed me

> *to preach good news to the poor.*
> *He has sent me to proclaim freedom for the prisoners*
>   *and recovery of sight for the blind,*
> *to release the oppressed,*
>   *to proclaim the year of the Lord's favour.*
>   (Luke 4:18–19, quoting Isaiah 61:1–2)

He read the ancient Hebrew words carefully and sat down to speak to the assembly in their own language, Aramaic. There was a pause as he glanced round the room, and then he said, *'Today this scripture is fulfilled in your hearing'* (verse 21).

This was an awkward moment. Here was the town carpenter making a bold claim to be the Messiah! There must have been a rustle of hostility, because Jesus didn't stop there. He went on to suggest that pagan Gentiles were better than God's people at recognizing God's messengers. The congregation felt insulted, and became violent. Jesus was hounded out by some regular synagogue-goers who wanted teach him a lesson. After this he moved to Capernaum. In future, his visits home would need to be cautious ones.

A people divided

Working out of Capernaum, and preaching in the open air to growing crowds, Jesus was addressing a divided and hurting community. The scrolls in the synagogue told them of a glorious past, when David and Solomon had fought off all comers. Now the land was split into administrative regions by the Roman conquerors, whose spies mingled with the crowds. Resistance to the rule of the emperor was dealt with simply. Rebels were nailed to a cross by their hands and feet and left to die in a suitably public place. Sometimes, so many people were crucified together that the soldiers ran out of wood.

Imagine you are a news reporter, working on a feature on this young and radical preacher. As the crowd waits for him to turn up, you mingle, interviewing as many people as you can. After a while, it becomes clear that there are several distinct groups present. That night you file your story. It might read something like this:

News of Jesus' visit to the small town of Magdala on the western shore of the Sea of Galilee brought the whole population out to wait for his arrival. Moving among the crowd, I could see why many of them had trudged so far. Around me were people with the kinds of diseases that are all too common in Galilee, all of them beyond the reach of the doctor's art, even if they could afford to pay for it. Most of them can't, of course. Jesus is the last resort of the poor and desperate. They are waiting for a miracle cure, but others have turned out to hear Jesus the teacher. There is a huge appetite for hope among the demoralized masses here in eastern Galilee. The work is hard, taxes are high and, underneath the sullen obedience offered to the Romans, rebellion is seething.

But this is a people divided, and unlikely to offer any unified threat to the empire. I spoke to an arrogant young man who obviously felt he belonged to an elite brotherhood. He was a Pharisee, and proud of it. He said that only his sect could interpret the law of Moses so that ordinary people could live in obedience to the will of God. They had, he said, developed additional laws that interpreted the ancient commands, so that the people knew exactly what to do and when to do it. The Pharisees live under a rigorous interpretation of the law, and that's how they expect everyone else to live.

Yet even among people who love the Torah there is disagreement. I met a fashionable couple who regarded themselves as direct descendants of the priests of ancient Israel, and who felt they had more right to interpret the law than had the Pharisees. They called themselves Sadducees, and said many of the Jewish aristocracy belong to their group. They smiled haughtily when I asked them about the Pharisees, mocking their primitive belief that there is life after death, yet confessing that the two groups had to work together to present a united front to the Romans. Their presence showed that Jesus had caught the attention of the establishment. I even saw official scribes present, preparing to write down what he said. The couple thought Jesus was probably a good influence; they felt sorry for the poor and hoped he would he would heal them.

Not all those present belonged to the establishment, though. Some of the Zealots had come out of the wilderness and were mingling with the crowd. As you would expect, they were passionate about the law, but couldn't compromise on the belief that the people of Israel should be free from Gentile oppression. These people are basically freedom fighters, visiting God's judgment (as they see it) on Israel's enemies. To be fair, they are also thieves and brigands, but you have to admire their courage.

It is hard not to admire the Essenes, too. I spoke to two monks from their desert community near the Dead Sea. They clearly have an affinity with both Jesus and John the Baptist, but would not say whether either of them was a member of their sect. For the Essenes, the essence of the law is the command to be holy, and they feel that the best way to achieve this is by getting away from the rest of us to live in their secretive community by the Salt Sea.

It would be wrong to leave you with the impression that everyone here is committed to some religious system. Far from it. Most people I spoke to in this crowd were only dimly aware of religious issues. These are the despised 'people of the land'. Some are Jews and others Gentiles, but none of them are committed to observing the law. The religious people present were concerned that Jesus was spending too much time with these people, and therefore making himself unclean. Yet, though some of them criticize Jesus, there is a lot of goodwill towards him. All the groups I spoke to are hopeful that this young rabbi from Nazareth will advance their own cause.

The beginnings of a team

It was by the lakeside that Jesus began to assemble a group of serious followers. In Matthew's account, he simply walks up to two brothers, Simon and Andrew, and out of the blue tells them to follow him. As if under a spell, they obey, and we are left marvelling at why these men should go off with a perfect stranger like this. As if this were not enough, Jesus does the same to James and John, the sons of the delightfully named Zebedee.

This is, of course, a one-dimensional picture. To get the

four-sided view, we need to look at this event in all four Gospels.

Luke hints that Jesus was lodging with Simon the fisherman before his call to be a disciple (Luke 4:38). He certainly healed Simon's mother-in-law of a raging fever (verse 39), so perhaps the fisherman thought he owed Jesus something. The extra attention generated by healings like this created a problem; Jesus did not want his healing ministry to overshadow his preaching. So he began to travel to other settlements to teach there too, staying one step ahead of the crowds. Mark records a remarkable saying of Jesus from around this time. As he is made aware that a huge crowd is searching for him, he says, *'Let us go somewhere else – to the nearby villages – so that I can preach there also. That is why I have come'* (Mark 1:38). As much as Jesus wanted to heal people, he was prepared to walk away from the crowds if their intensity prevented him from teaching.

In this way Jesus gradually covered Galilee with his influence, while regularly returning to Bethsaida or Capernaum. It was here that Simon and his brother Andrew worked in close partnership with their friends James and John. By the time Jesus challenged them to follow him, they knew pretty well what they were getting themselves into.

Luke tells us even more about why Peter decided to leave his career and throw in his lot with Jesus. We will look at this in a moment. But first, let's indulge in a spot of marine archaeology.

How to catch a fisherman

In January 1986, two brothers, Moshe and Yuval Lufan, from the Kibbutz Ginosar on the western shore of Lake

Galilee, found an elongated oval outline in the mud a few hundred metres from their home. They were often out scavenging for coins and ancient artefacts, and, as the drought that year had lowered the water level drastically, they had been searching a part of the shoreline never before prospected by archaeologists. The Department of Antiquities was called in and the area was investigated by professionals. Moshe and Yuval had found an ancient fishing-boat which radio-carbon dating confirmed was in use on the lake during the lifetime of Jesus and his disciples.

The boat was quite big: 8.2 metres long and 2.3 metres wide. The planks were skilfully joined edge to edge, with no overlaps, by special mortise-and-tenon joints. The skill of the carpenters who built it was astonishing, considering the tools they had at their disposal. These workmen could produce sophisticated work, it seems. Indeed, the boat itself had been carefully repaired many times during its working life, and in the end was being used for spare parts for other boats. A little oil lamp was found on board, the sort that Jesus sometimes used as an illustration in his talks.

There is no way of knowing whether this boat is one of those that put in an appearance in the Gospels, but the find helps us to see that the boats of Galilee were first-rate fishing-platforms that were big enough to be adapted for other jobs. Jesus spent a lot of time in boats like these, but he had developed a very different use for them.

Luke describes Jesus borrowing a boat like this in order to teach the crowds without being mobbed. He addressed the crowds from the boat, and everyone sat on the shore to listen. The boat was Simon's and, at the end of the session, Jesus suggested to him that they went fishing. Being a professional, Simon was not keen. He had been fishing nearby all night and had caught nothing. In his judgment, an extra trip was going to be a waste of time. In Luke's carefully written account of this, Peter shows his respect for Jesus by being willing to humour his request and by the way he addresses Jesus: *'Master, we've worked hard all night and haven't caught anything. But because you say so, I will let down the nets'* (Luke 5:5).

Simon was in for a huge surprise. The nets came up so full of fish that he had to call in other boats to handle the catch. Soon James and John were alongside, helping him to cope. But Simon had more than a logistics problem on his mind. It slowly dawned on him that there was no natural explanation for what was happening. (You may feel otherwise, but Peter was a professional, remember!) He began to see that the person in the boat with him was more than an ordinary rabbi. At that moment, Simon knelt down and spoke to Jesus: *'Go away from me, Lord'*, he said; *'I am a sinful man!'* (verse 8).

Simon, who had so far called Jesus 'master', now addressed him quite differently as 'Lord'. The word 'Lord' was a common term of respect towards people in authority, but it could be used of God also. Later in the same chapter Luke says, *'The power of the Lord* [God] *was present for him* [Jesus] *to heal the sick'* (verse 17). Yet the word 'Lord' is less significant than what Simon *did*, and than what he obviously thought; he felt he was too sinful to be in Jesus' company, and he knelt down in reverence to speak to him. This is a strange way to address a friend, even if he was an especially impressive rabbi.

This climax to the story echoes an Old Testament incident. The great prophet Isaiah saw a vision of God in the temple and fell to his knees just like Simon. This ancient resonance of Luke's description, and the astonishing reaction of Simon himself, draw us to question whether we are dealing with a mere human being at all. Is Jesus more than a teacher?

For Simon and his friends, that question was at least partly answered. They had some appreciation that Jesus was in some way very different from any prophet that had gone before. It was at this moment that Jesus chose to make his challenge: *'Come, follow me,'* he said, *'From now on you will catch men'* (Mark 1:17; Luke 5:10). The disciples pulled their boats up the beach and put their fishing careers on ice for the time being.

Wider influence

Herod's little province of Galilee was, as we have seen, well connected with the rest of the region. Rumours about Jesus spread quickly, and soon people from other provinces joined the Galilean crowds. Some of them were pretty desperate, and Matthew lists people with severe pain, seizures and paralysis being brought by friends and family to see if Jesus could heal them (Matthew 4:23–25). The impression you get from reading the Gospels is that each and every one Jesus touched was instantly and completely made well. This being the case, Simon's conviction that Jesus was more than human must have grown.

But is there another explanation for these miracle stories? Were Matthew and his colleagues exaggerating Jesus' powers? Was Jesus able occasionally to improve the physical condition of some of his followers through psychological means, which seemed impressive in a pre-scientific society? As the stories were told and retold, were they embellished and made to sound more dramatic?

It is undeniable that Jesus was drawing huge crowds; people were prepared to travel long distances to hear him. What was the attraction, I wonder? An interesting series of talks about ethics and a few dubious healings? I suspect not! His miracles made such an impact that early enemies of Christianity couldn't deny that they had happened. After all, too many people had seen Jesus in action. They preferred to put Jesus' power down to sorcery rather than to the power of God. The fact that his early critics found the miracles undeniable is powerful evidence that something more than words kick-started the Jesus movement.

The controversial disciple

Crossing the borders of the small provinces that fringed the Sea of Galilee was expensive. If you travelled from the Decapolis and crossed the Jordan into Galilee, you would have to pay a tax on any goods you brought into the country to sell. It was the same if you came up from Samaria or down from Syria. A familiar sight in those parts was the tax collector, or *publicanus*, sitting in his little hut by the roadside taking revenues for the tetrarch, and, if contemporary stories are to be believed, a little something for himself too.

In fact, 'tax collector' was a term of abuse, along with 'prostitute' and 'sinner'. They were often dishonest, and they were linked with the Roman occupying forces. The general public saw them as traitors and scum, and deeply religious Jews felt that their regular contact with Gentiles made them religiously polluted and unacceptable to God. Lots of Jesus' visitors would have to pass by these tax collectors as they crossed the border; many of them would have been searched and even fleeced by them. It is not hard to imagine the feelings of hatred towards these Jewish representatives of the Roman empire.

Yet it is at this time in Jesus' life that Luke describes him walking up to one of these tax farmers in his customs post and inviting him to become one of his team (see Luke 5:27–32). His name was Levi, and he must have been itching to get out of his corrupt career and break free, because he simply abandoned his desk and joined the team without a moment's hesitation. Later on, Levi invited a crowd of people back to his house for a meal, and everyone enjoyed the occasion. Levi had something to celebrate; a dark phase of his life was over and he wanted to party!

But Levi's friends were a motley crew, and few of them took religion seriously. To religious Jews it was not acceptable behaviour to eat with people like this, for it polluted you in God's sight. So the Pharisees got hold of Simon and his friends and attacked them and their leader: *'Why do you eat and drink with tax collectors and "sinners"?'* (Luke 5:30) Some of Jesus' friends may have thought the same. Ordinary people hated the likes of Levi.

Maintaining the religious status quo was the Pharisees' goal in life. As long as Jesus went along with this, they would be happy. His impressive performance in Galilee could only do good. But it was important to keep up the standards the Pharisees had set to guide the people in their religion. If Jesus wanted to be a guide too, then he would have to be like them. Jesus had stepped out of line by eating with the kind of people a rabbi shouldn't mix with, so it was the responsibility of those who were more righteous to get him to see the error of his ways.

Jesus' answer to their criticism came as a shock: *'I have not come to call the righteous, but sinners to repentance.'* Whatever Jesus had to offer, it was going to be available to outsiders like Levi as well as to nice middle-class people like Simon and his friends. This didn't seem right to the Pharisees; Jesus would have to be watched more closely.

6

What was Jesus saying?

1. The Sermon on the Mount

In 1989 the Communist regimes of Eastern Europe were falling apart. As the year drew to a close, that great symbol of Europe's division, the Berlin Wall, was torn down. In the months that followed, some of East Germany's old communist leaders were put on trial for serious crimes. One of these was the ex-President, Erich Honecker. He had made life tough for East Germany's Christians, and some had even experienced physical persecution because of their faith. Those who hadn't nevertheless faced the relentless opposition of the state: promising students couldn't get jobs; gifted workers couldn't get promotion; brilliant academics could survive only by doing menial work. When the wall came down, there were lots of good reasons to get even with people like Honecker. So when he fell from high office, was arrested and was awaiting trial, it delighted his many enemies that he was alone and without a place to live. It was then that a Christian leader called Uwe Holmer stepped in.

Despite the outrage of the press and of many who had suffered at the hands of the former President, Uwe Holmer took Dr and Mrs Honecker into his family home and sheltered them. It wasn't long before Erich Honecker became seriously ill, dying of cancer a few months later. But during those last months of his life, this scourge of the East German church was loved and nursed by one of that church's leaders.

Jesus' words in the Sermon on the Mount, *'Love your enemies and pray for those who persecute you'* (Matthew 5:44), have influenced the world. Mahatma Gandhi, who led the powerful non-violent independence movement in India, once wrote that the Sermon on the Mount 'dominated his heart'. Even if the only recorded words of Jesus had been his Sermon on the Mount, he would surely still have made a deep impact on history.

Valley deep or mountain high?

Is the Sermon on the Mount, as reported in Matthew, a transcript of a speech Jesus made? Or is it more of a compilation of pieces of ethical teaching written up as though it was one talk? Most scholars think it is the second. There are some good reasons for this view. Most important is the fact that the Sermon on the Mount appears in a different form in Luke's Gospel, where it is set instead on a low-lying plain, and Jesus is said to go down with the disciples, instead of up as in Matthew (see Luke 6:17; Matthew 5:1). It looks as though Luke took roughly the same material, stripped out the Jewish references that his Greek readers would not understand, and set it down in a different way.

Whether the Sermon is a compilation or a transcript is really unimportant. There may well have been both a

Sermon on the Mount and a Sermon on the Plain. Jesus was a brilliant communicator, as well as a travelling preacher. He would have had the skill to recast Jewish material for an audience of Gentiles, and he undoubtedly had to do this from time to time. Travelling preachers are always adapting illustrations and parables to new groups of people. (I know this because I am one myself.) This explains why readers of the Gospels come across similar teaching in different settings. The writer didn't get it wrong; that's just how preachers work.

The Sermon on the Mount has a definite purpose. Jesus was clearly setting out to challenge the religious assumptions of his listeners and to show us how we can enjoy intimacy with God. The key to this is what he called 'righteousness', that is, living in line with the will of God. The Sermon on the Mount sets out to answer the question, 'How can we be righteous people?'

The desire to live a righteous life united Jesus' hearers. They may have had different ways of interpreting their Torah, but they were agreed that God had spoken through it and that it was the key to righteousness. In the Sermon on the Mount, Jesus was inviting them to think in a completely new way about this.

Getting the world's attention

Let's assume that Matthew's record of the Sermon on the Mount is a transcript or a summary of the original message. Jesus began with short, proverb-like verses. Perhaps he paused after each one to let it sink in, because these ideas were quite new and were intended to be puzzling and thought-provoking. *'Blessed are the poor in spirit, for theirs is the kingdom of heaven'* (Matthew 5:3). His hearers must have wondered exactly what he meant by 'poor in spirit': was he talking about being economically challenged, or some other kind of poverty?

As they were thinking, he continued: *'Blessed are those who mourn, for they will be comforted'* (verse 4). Now that was easier; he was offering some kind of comfort to grieving people. But some of Jesus' sayings went against common sense; for instance: *'Blessed are the meek, for they will inherit the earth'* (verse 5). In first-century Palestine might was right. The only way the meek could inherit the earth would be to challenge the rule of the powerful, and even then they could hope to inherit only about six feet of it!

Proverb by proverb, Jesus must have talked his audience into attentive silence. His words have mesmerized people ever since. Today we call these proverbs 'the Beatitudes'.

'Beatitude' is a word derived from the Latin *beatus*, meaning 'happy'. At first sight, then, Jesus was offering a recipe for happiness. But here we come up against a problem of translation. The word 'happy' suggests feeling ecstatic and carefree, but for the New Testament writers feelings didn't really come into it. They saw 'blessedness' as a lifestyle that bore God's approval, and which led to contentment whatever the circumstances. If you are merely happy, your *joie de vivre* will evaporate if something nasty happens; but if you are blessed you can still know contentment at the deepest level.

The Beatitudes paint a powerful and challenging picture of the way we could be, but they don't offer a quick route to personal peace. They end with the chilling prospect that those who commit themselves to a lifestyle that Jesus calls 'righteousness' will be victimized and discriminated against because of it: *'Blessed are you when people insult you, persecute you, and falsely say all kinds of evil against you because of me. Rejoice and be glad, because great is your reward in heaven'* (verses 11–12).

From the beginning, Jesus stresses that he is not calling us to a private spirituality, or prescribing a religious tonic that will help us to feel better and nothing more. Instead, he called those first hearers to a make public commitment to him personally, and to live their lives of righteousness openly so that others could see how they too should live: *'Let your light shine before men, that they may see your good deeds and praise your Father in heaven'* (verse 16).

'Tick the box' religion

Perhaps Jesus often repeated the Beatitudes (or similar sayings) to get the attention of crowds, encouraging them to begin to focus on issues bigger than healing. As these short sayings brought the crowd to an attentive quiet, Jesus began to talk about the law: *'Do not think that I have come to abolish the Law or the Prophets; I have not come to abolish them but to fulfil them'* (verse 17).

His listeners would have felt reassured: Jesus would never seek to reject the Torah. But something about his words must have left them feeling uneasy. 'What did he mean, he would fulfil the law?' What followed was an exposé of the weakness and hypocrisy with which his critics used the Torah: *'Unless your righteousness surpasses that of the Pharisees and the teachers of the law, you will certainly not enter the kingdom of heaven.'* (verse 20).

This bombshell introduced six attacks on the Pharisees' method (verses 21–48). In each of these test cases, Jesus insisted that real righteousness is not a matter of wooden obedience to the letter of the law – much less to the law as embellished by the Pharisees. (Leviticus 19:18, quoted in verse 43, does not say 'and hate your enemy'.) Rather, it means getting at the heart of each commandment and living it out in your life.

Here's an example.

> *'You have heard that it was said, "Do not commit adultery." But I tell you that anyone who looks at a woman lustfully has already committed adultery with her in his heart. If your right eye causes you to sin, gouge it out and throw it away. It is better for you to lose one part of your body than for your whole body to be thrown into hell. And if your right hand causes you to sin, cut it off and throw it away. It is better for you to lose one part of your body than for your whole body to go into hell'* (Matthew 5:27–30).

This was a radical challenge to the law-obsessed religious leaders of Judea, who measured their spiritual progress by mentally ticking off the Old Testament laws like items on a 'to do' list. On that level it was quite easy to keep the seventh commandment, *'You shall not commit adultery.'* But Jesus insisted that the spirit of the law is equally important. Real righteousness is not just a matter of not going to bed with the wrong people, but about the way we look at each other – whether our glances value or cheapen the one glanced at.

Most religions run on the principle that you please God by ticking off his commandments, and some Jews regarded their own religion in this way too. There's a striking example of this in one of the letters of Paul, an early Christian leader who started out as Saul of Tarsus, a member of the Pharisee group. He speaks about deriving huge spiritual satisfaction from his Jewish pedigree and religious performance:

> *If anyone else thinks he has reasons to put confidence in the flesh, I have more: circumcised on the eighth*

day, of the people of Israel, of the tribe of Benjamin, a
Hebrew of Hebrews; in regard to the law, a Pharisee;
as for zeal, persecuting the church; as for legalistic
righteousness, faultless (Philippians 3:4–6).

As you read this, you can imagine the Pharisee ticking
the boxes. Paul had regarded himself as faultless because he
had not actually broken any of the commandments. He
had not murdered, committed adultery or broken an oath.
His sense of righteousness was, as he put it, legalistic. Yet
there was something wrong: this religious paragon was
active in oppressing people whose ideas were different
from his. On the outside, things were fine, but inside he
was filled with hatred, malice and violence.

Jesus was attacking the complacency of people like this,
who were righteous by the standard of a rigid set of rules,
but whose rules didn't touch the pollution present in the
human heart. In time, Paul came to understand righteousness in this way too, and he explained the change in the
letter I quoted just now:

But whatever was to my profit I now consider loss for
the sake of Christ. What is more, I consider everything
a loss compared to the surpassing greatness of knowing
Christ Jesus my Lord, for whose sake I have lost all
things (Philippians 3:7–8).

The challenge of the Sermon on the Mount is to live
for God. It's about going deeper than mere rule-keeping. It
means becoming passionate about inner change. Jesus
himself put it like this: *'Blessed are those who hunger and*
thirst for righteousness, for they will be filled' (Matthew 5:6).

Beyond the law

Of course, all that box-ticking makes people proud. Jesus moves on to attack religious pride next. *'Be careful'*, he said, *'not to do your "acts of righteousness" before men, to be seen by them. If you do, you will have no reward from your Father in heaven'* (Matthew 6:1).

The Pharisees' showy pride as they prayed, fasted and made their gifts in the temple was exposed as a sham. The admiring glances of the too easily impressed passers-by were all the reward they could expect for their pains. Once more, Jesus' words boil down to a challenge to learn that serving God was not about religious box-ticking, but about an inner longing to know God and to be inwardly transformed by him. That's why he tells us to do our acts of righteousness in secret, so that only God will know. The reward can then be left safely in God's hands.

In Jesus' thinking, righteousness leads to a reward which is building up for us in heaven, the home of God and the ultimate home of those who treasure God above all else. It is hard to imagine the nature of the reward that Jesus had in mind, but this is one of those issues he left to our imagination. More important for the here and now is question of where we would rather accumulate our treasure.

At the heart of all this lies the question: What do I treasure most? If we love wealth, power and status above everything, then this will determine our actions throughout our life. The tragedy, according to Jesus, is that these things are fragile and can so easily be lost. But if we love God more than everything, and we seek his approval and blessing in all we do, we have something that can never be lost, for they are indestructible. Where *does* our real treasure lie? Jesus rounds off this challenge with the uncompromising statement: *'You cannot serve both God and Money'* (6:24).

The Sermon on the Mount is full of sharp challenges about the way we think and live. Yet it would be a mistake to get the impression that it is all like this. Some of Jesus' most famous sayings focus on encouraging people who feel fragile and fearful: *'Why do you worry about clothes? See how the lilies of the field grow. They do not labour or spin. Yet I tell you that not even Solomon in all his splendour was dressed like one of these'* (Matthew 6:28–29). People who make the kingdom of God their priority, Jesus said, will not need to worry about life's necessities; God will look after them.

Yet the main point of the Sermon on the Mount is to force rigorous self-examination on its hearers and readers. How many of our conversations revolve around other people's failings? We feel smug when we compare ourselves with others who seem to have made a bigger mess of things than we have. Jesus piles in with the warning that this kind of hypocrisy will one day rebound on us: *'In the same way as you judge others, you will be judged, and with the measure you use, it will be measured to you'* (Matthew 7:2).

Imagine going through life with a digital recorder taped to your chest. Each time you say something about someone else, it records what you say. Every unkind word and thoughtless judgment is preserved. At the end of time, the recorder plays it all back to you. Can you imagine how embarrassing that would be? Jesus says that our judgments on others will form the basis of the way God evaluates us.

The kind of transformation Jesus is pushing us towards will change not only the way we treat people but also the way we speak of them. His famous 'golden rule' summarizes this in one simple proverb: *'In everything, do to others what you would have them do to you, for this sums up the Law and the Prophets'* (Matthew 7:12).

Something strong to build your life on

The Beatitudes had made a dramatic start, and God's law had been the main point of the talk. You would expect a nice story at the end, encouraging people to go home and to try very hard to live good lives, to be nice to each other and to go to synagogue regularly. To people expecting an ethical challenge, Jesus had a surprise in store. Instead of an appeal to turn over a new leaf and live better lives from now on, Jesus chose to invite people to make a personal response to him as God's authoritative messenger, and to build their lives on his words. 'Don't just follow the crowd,' he says (Matthew 7:13–14). 'And don't listen to every religious teacher you hear' he adds (Matthew 7:15–23). The punchline of the Sermon on the Mount tells the story of two people who each build a house, and reveals Jesus' understanding of himself:

> *'Therefore everyone who hears these words of mine and puts them into practice is like a wise man who built his house on the rock. The rain came down, the streams rose, and the winds blew and beat against that house; yet it did not fall, because it had its foundation on the rock. But everyone who hears these words of mine and does not put them into practice is like a foolish man who built his house on sand. The rain came down, the streams rose, and the winds blew and beat against that house, and it fell with a great crash'* (Matthew 7:24–27).

The final challenge of the Sermon on the Mount is to build your life on Jesus and his teaching. Jesus had left his hearers in no doubt about one thing: he was unlike anyone they had ever seen or heard before. *'When Jesus had finished saying these things, the crowds were amazed at his teaching, because he taught as one who had authority, and not as their teachers of the law'* (7:28–29).

It does not take much effort to see how the relevance of the Sermon on the Mount comes screaming like an express train right into the twenty-first century. Can the Kosovo Albanians forgive their Serbian neighbours? Is there a satisfying way to live outside the materialist rat-race? Can I remedy the flaws in my character that make relationships with others so difficult? All these issues are addressed in different ways by Jesus' words. He affirmed that God really had spoken in the Torah, and he modelled a challenging new way of interpreting its heart. He dismissed the complacency of the tick-the-box religious, and insisted on heart-level change. We all need something solid to build our lives on, and Jesus said that he is that something solid.

Well, he could certainly talk; there is no doubt about that! The question remained, however: how could he back up his claims to such massive authority?

7
Jesus on the move

Mahatma Gandhi led the movement to secure India's independence from British rule in the 1940s. One of his most dramatic showdowns with the British Raj was a long walk from Ahmdabad to the Arabian Sea, where he collected sea-water and evaporated it to make salt in defiance of British law. The Raj had placed a tax on salt production, a commodity no-one could do without. Indian resentment demanded a powerful protest. In Richard Attenborough's film of Gandhi's life, there is a dramatic sequence showing the tiny, bald-headed hero striding through rural India gathering followers as he went. The climax comes as they reach the sea and the inevitable confrontation with British imperialism.

There's something of this atmosphere in Luke's Gospel as Jesus sets out decisively to walk from Galilee to Jerusalem for the last time. Wherever he goes there are crowds, and expectations are running high. When he arrives in Jerusalem he announces his presence by turfing the money-changers out of their place of work in the sacred precincts of the temple. Jews visiting from all over the world had to change money in order to buy animals to sacrifice, but local profiteers had turned the place into a 'den of robbers'. The way Luke tells it, you know a storm is brewing (see Luke 19:45–48).

Matthew tells us about the same journey, but arranges the incidents in a different order. After months of work in Galilee, people were beginning to notice that Jesus *spoke* with great authority (see the comments Matthew reports at the end of the Sermon on the Mount, Matthew 7:28–29). In the chapters that follow, Matthew deliberately grouped together accounts of incidents that show Jesus as one who *acted* with great authority, and indicates that his actions gave authority to his teaching. Near the beginning of the sequence is an incident in which a senior Roman soldier comes to him for help, acknowledging Jesus' immense authority (Matthew 8:5–13). The sequence ends with Jesus delegating his authority to his team so that they can go and do similar things (Matthew 10:1).

This difference in the use of the journey motif in Luke and in Matthew illustrates the fact that the Gospels are structured in different ways, and do not pay too much attention to the exact sequence of events. Nevertheless, all the Gospel writers indicate that, after these early successes in Galilee, Jesus was on the move. His base remained in Capernaum, but he was travelling more frequently and more widely, occasionally venturing into Gentile areas such as the Decapolis, and regularly visiting Jerusalem for certain Jewish feasts. Throughout this period he continued to show a preference for working in rural areas rather than the bigger cities, and for the most part his priority was to take his message to Jews rather than to Gentiles.

It was a period of intensive activity and almost constant

movement. Although Jesus had some kind of home in Capernaum, he once said with feeling, *'Foxes have holes and birds of the air have nests, but the Son of Man has nowhere to lay his head'* (Matthew 8:20). Anyone whose job involves frequent travel will know exactly how Jesus must have felt.

A day in the life ...

Jesus began each day by finding somewhere quiet where he could pray. A man who loved people deeply, he also loved solitude. As his popularity began to put pressure on his time, he would get up while it was still dark and look for somewhere to be alone. Sometimes his friends had trouble finding him first thing in the morning (Mark 1:35–39).

His preaching programme meant frequent walks on the dirt roads that criss-crossed the region. Most days would involve travel in the company of his close friends and followers. Simon and his brother Andrew were always with him, as were James and John, but during this time Jesus was adding to his group of disciples. We have already seen him recruiting Levi, and in the course of his travels he gathered seven more men to make a squad of twelve.

In Jesus' world it would have been outrageous for a rabbi to appoint women as his disciples. Nevertheless, there was a significant group of women in his entourage. Luke mentions three in particular, one of whom was Joanna, the wife of Herod Antipas' household manager, presumably an aristocratic woman with some wealth behind her. Of the other two, Mary Magdalene is worth a mention. Her name indicates that she came from the village of Magdala on the western edge of the Sea of Galilee. History and romantic tradition have tainted her memory, and she is often spoken of as having been a prostitute. There is no evidence that this was the case.

Each day's walking would be in the company of a group of men and women who felt a strong commitment to Jesus' cause. But there was a cost to this. His team of disciples was now with Jesus constantly; they had apparently left their work behind and didn't have an income to support themselves or their families. The three women mentioned by Luke were helping out financially by supporting the team out of their own means (Luke 8:1–3).

Not everybody could cope with this lifestyle, though many thought they could. People would offer themselves to Jesus as disciples, but he was quite short with most of them. The Gospels record some hard questions that Jesus fired at those who fancied going on the road with him (for example, Matthew 8:18–22). This didn't stop people tagging along for the ride and joining him for sections of the journey. As they walked the roads of Galilee, people would come and go, some staying for a few hours and others for days.

Sometimes the disciples would travel separately in pairs sent ahead of the main group, to prepare these villages for Jesus' arrival. On other occasions the whole group would fan out across the region, getting practical experience in preaching and beginning to learn how to communicate the message of the kingdom for themselves. These were intense times, and the teams would return exhausted.

Often, they could not get the rest they needed. Jesus' success generated such huge interest that he couldn't escape the crowds. Mark passes on Simon Peter's recollection of returning from a two-man mission to the villages of Galilee, only to find that people were coming to Jesus in such numbers that they couldn't find time to eat, let alone sleep. Anxious to get some breathing-space for his people, and some solitude to debrief them, Jesus got his friends into the nearest boat and they rowed to a quiet beach nearby. But they had been observed. As they rowed in to land the boat, they were dismayed to see that the crowds had arrived ahead of them (Mark 6:30–33).

It sounds like a bad day at the office. You are trying to get an important job done and people won't let you. Yet Jesus' response to the people was impressive. I would have been screaming with frustration, but he *'had compassion on them, because they were like sheep without a shepherd. So he began teaching them many things'* (verse 34). Characteristically, though the crowds were probably there to see something spectacular happen, Jesus began to teach them. Once again he restates the importance of seeing him as a teacher as well as a wonder-worker.

By the time Jesus had finished, it was very late. People were tired and a long way from home. There were about five thousand men in the crowd, and some had their families with them. Children were crying for something to eat, and their mothers were worried that the walk home on an empty stomach would be a miserable affair. In their excitement to get to see Jesus, their preparations for the trip had been skimpy. In their fascination with what he had to say, they had forgotten the passage of time. What a riveting teacher this Jesus must have been!

No-one was about to starve, but the place was remote and they had an uncomfortable journey ahead of them. Those people now needed something more than a sermon. The disciples were relaying the people's anxiety to Jesus and telling him they had only a few loaves of bread and some fish. Jesus took the food and said the traditional Jewish thanksgiving over it. Then he divided the paltry amount between his disciples, who moved out among the crowd distributing it. As they did so, the bread and the fish multiplied. Every outstretched hand was filled, every hungry child was satisfied, and everyone ate their fill. Collecting up the leftovers afterwards, the disciples counted twelve big basketfuls of fish and bread pieces.

It had been a long day. The disciples had to get back to Bethsaida, where some of them had homes. They didn't fancy a night out in the open. So, as Jesus watched the crowds drift away into the gathering darkness, his friends piled into the boat for the long row home. Alone on the hillside above the lake, Jesus knelt down and finished the day as he had begun it, in prayer.

The 'Son of Man'

Jesus did not always teach in the open air. He frequently used someone's house, or, if it was the Sabbath, a synagogue. But venues like this could cause problems for the public, and all three synoptic writers record what happened when he was teaching in his home town of Capernaum (Matthew 9:2–7; Mark 2:3–12; Luke 5:18–25). It was a tense occasion because a number of Pharisees were present, some of whom had come up from Jerusalem to see what Jesus was getting up to.

The room was jammed to capacity, and people crowded round the doors and windows trying to catch what was being said in the house. This was difficult because of loud hammering noises coming from the roof. As Jesus spoke, the teachers from the Jerusalem temple weighed every word, scanning each phrase for heresy.

Suddenly, the flat roof fell in, covering Jesus and his examiners in dust and plaster.

Looking up at the blue sky framed by a large hole in the ceiling, Jesus could see four faces, and then the underside of a makeshift stretcher being lowered through the hole. People squeezed back so that it could come to rest in front of Jesus. On it lay a man with a hopeful expression in his eyes. His body was motionless from the neck downwards. Someone in the room was shouting at the men on the roof, demanding to know who would pay for the damage. Jesus looked at the man and spoke to him: *'Son, your sins are forgiven.'*

There was silence in the room, the kind you get when someone has said something embarrassing and nobody knows how to restore the atmosphere. Jesus looked at the Pharisees, who had begun to mutter to each other. 'You think I'm blaspheming, don't you?' he said. 'Because only God can forgive sins.' The men from Jerusalem nodded silently, and the man on the stretcher looked less hopeful. He wondered what sins he was supposed to have committed when he couldn't even move his limbs. 'Let me prove to you' Jesus said, 'That I am the Son of Man, and that I do indeed have the authority to forgive sins.' He turned to the paraplegic man on the stretcher. 'Get up, and take your stretcher and go home.' And the man did exactly what he was told. Without hesitation, he stood up. As people rubbed their eyes in disbelief, he left the room.

What a strange title, *the Son of Man*! Jesus referred to himself as the Son of Man many times (about seventy-five times in the Gospels) but no-one else ever did. On the face of it he was stating the obvious, like a tadpole calling itself the Son of Frog. In fact, it is more significant than this.

It is a two-way title, which hints at both deity and humanity. The phrase crops up occasionally in the Old Testament and simply means 'human beings' (see for example Psalm 8). Tucked away towards the end of the Old Testament, however, is the book of Daniel, and here 'the Son of Man' is more than merely human:

> '*In my vision at night I looked, and there before me was one like a son of man, coming with the clouds of heaven. He approached the Ancient of Days and was led into his presence. He was given authority, glory and sovereign power; all peoples, nations and men of every language worshipped him. His dominion is an everlasting dominion that will not pass away, and his kingdom is one that will never be destroyed* (Daniel 7:13–14).

This Son of Man is obviously a very glorious figure indeed, and the fact that he is legitimately being worshipped indicates that he is in some way divine. Jesus' repeated use of this title for himself emphasized both his humanity and his claim to heavenly authority. This was a huge claim for him to make, but it was hard for his audience to deny it. They had just seen the proof walk out of the door carrying his own stretcher.

Faith and unbelief

When he looked up at the structural damage done by the four friends of the paraplegic, Jesus saw more than four grinning faces. He recognized that their vandalism stemmed from a deep belief that he could heal their friend. '*When Jesus saw their faith, he said to the paralytic, "Take heart, son; your sins are forgiven"*' (Matthew 9:2). Faith was the response that Jesus was looking for everywhere he went. When people didn't believe, he didn't work miracles.

Matthew (13:53–58) recalls a disastrous return visit to Nazareth to teach in the synagogue. It wasn't long before the townsfolk were up in arms against Jesus because they simply could not bring themselves to accept that someone they knew so well could have such authority. The comment Jesus made on leaving the town has entered our everyday language as a proverb: 'A prophet is without honour in his own country.' Yet it is the sentence that follows that is more important: *'He did not do many miracles there because of their lack of faith'* (verse 58). Jesus was asking people to respond to his authority by believing in him, and to realize that when he worked in their lives it was in response to faith.

Around this time, a local dignitary, Jairus, approached Jesus with a request to come quickly, for his little daughter was dying (Mark 5:21–43). The group swiftly changed course and headed for the official's house. But on the way a woman with a haemorrhage touched Jesus' cloak, thinking that if only she could do so she too would be healed. Jesus swung round and asked who had touched him. He kept looking around, waiting for an answer. When it came, Jesus said to the woman, *'Your faith has healed you'.* It was vital for Jesus that nobody went away with the illusion that they had been healed as if by magic. No, the Son of Man had responded to their faith in him by exercising his divine power. This was not magic; God was at work.

The interruption meant that precious time was lost on the urgent visit to the agonized official's house. While Jesus was dealing with the woman, the message came that the little girl had in fact died. Jesus calmed the distraught father and continued on his way. When he reached Jairus' house, he was taken to the dead girl. He took her cold hand and quietly spoke to her in Aramaic, *'Talitha koum!'* It means, *'Little girl … get up!'* and that's what she did. Jesus suggested that they give her something to eat, and added that he would like them to keep the incident as quiet as possible.

This was an almost impossible request, because people knew that the girl had died, and would see that she was now alive. Yet this was not the only healing that Jesus had asked to be kept quiet. Naturally, he did not want to be mobbed by too many people, and rumours of dead people being raised could cause problems. But was there another reason?

The hidden Christ

The Neo-Impressionist painter Georges Seurat composed his pictures of tiny rectangular dots of colour. When you stand back, they suddenly come together to make a subtle image of reality. In the same way, each incident recorded in the Gospels builds up a portrait of someone who claimed divine authority and could back up that claim with his actions. But what was the final portrait going to depict? Would it be a prophet, an angel, a demon, or someone too exalted to imagine? Jesus seemed to be waiting for people to work out for themselves who he really was. They did not need to guess; they had only to listen to his words and to see his works to solve the riddle.

This is why Jesus' miracles are so important. If he had been only a challenging religious teacher, nobody would ever have guessed his real nature. Religious teachers are ten a penny in the history of the world. Jesus used miracles to force the question of his real identity and authority on to those who saw them. Speculation was rife, but the breakthrough came in the very north of Galilee, during a visit to the town of Caesarea Philippi (Matthew 16:13–20).

As the team talked together one day, Jesus asked them if they could tell him what the people of Galilee made of him. *'Who do people say the Son of Man is?'* He was wondering how close they were so solving the riddle.

The disciples' reply was fascinating: the locals reckoned that Jesus must be one of the great prophets of the past, reincarnated. The fact is that everybody knew by now that the only explanation for Jesus would be a supernatural one. People who had seen him in action knew he could not be merely human.

Jesus wondered if the penny had yet dropped with those who were closest to him, so he asked them: *'What about you? Who do you say I am?'*

I imagine they looked round at each other as groups of people always do when they are put on the spot. It was Simon Peter who spoke first: *'You are the Christ, the Son of the living God.'*

It was a decisive moment. For Peter and his friends, the dots had coalesced into a coherent picture, and, from that point on, Jesus was open with his close friends about what it meant that he was 'the Christ' (the Greek term for the Hebrew title 'the Messiah').

To the Jews, the Messiah was the long-promised king who would rescue Israel from their enemies, and in Jesus' day that meant the Romans. This is probably what Simon Peter and his friends understood by the term. They probably had a vague idea that Jesus would lead an army into a great battle with Rome and restore the kingdom to Israel. This is the moment Jesus chose to re-educate his friends about the role of the Christ. Yes, there would be a battle, but there would be no army. The Messiah was going into single combat: *'From that time on Jesus began to explain to his disciples that he must go to Jerusalem and suffer many things at the hands of the elders, chief priests and teachers of the law, and that he must be killed and on the third day be raised to life'* (Matthew 16:21).

The other side of Jesus

Six days later, Jesus retreated to a nearby hilltop with his three closest associates, Simon Peter, James and John. Traditionally, this place is assumed to be Mount Tabor, a flat-topped hill in Galilee. The exact location is less significant than the strange event that took place there (Matthew 17:1–13).

Each of the Synoptic Gospels says that Jesus was 'transfigured' in front of his friends. Some kind of metamorphosis occurred, making it almost impossible to look at him directly. In Matthew's words, *'His face shone like the sun, and his clothes became as white as the light.'* As the terrified disciples looked on, they saw that he was deep in conversation with two people. They were Moses, the great lawgiver who led the people of Israel out of Egypt, and Elijah, one of the mightiest prophets of all time, and the one whose return was expected to precede the coming of the Messiah. As they conversed, a disembodied voice spoke to Peter, James and John: *'This is my son, whom I love; with him I am well pleased. Listen to him!'*

There is no doubt that the inclusion of this strongly supernatural story has stirred up some criticism of the Gospel writers. A lot of scholars insist that this has to be a mythical story and that no such event could ever have taken place. In the sceptical atmosphere of the twenty-first century it is tempting to agree. Yet it must have seemed as unreal to the first disciples when they experienced it as it does to us when we read about it. Peter came back to this incident in a letter he wrote to an early Christian group in Asia Minor:

> *We did not follow cleverly invented stories when we told you about the power and coming of our Lord Jesus*

Christ, but we were eye-witnesses of his majesty. For he received honour and glory from God the Father when the voice came to him from the Majestic Glory, saying 'This is my Son, whom I love; with him I am well pleased.' We ourselves heard this voice that came from heaven when we were with him on the sacred mountain (2 Peter 1:16–18).

It is as though Peter is saying, 'I know it is hard to believe, but we saw it.'

It's fascinating that all three Synoptic Gospels record the same sequence of events in Jesus' life at this stage. He was recognized as the Christ by his disciples; then he introduced them to the fact that he would be crucified in Jerusalem; and then he took the three disciples up the hill and was transfigured. This was clearly a very important event. The transfiguration took the screen away and revealed the other side of Jesus' nature, the more than human side. He is not only the Son of Man; he is the one and only Son of the one and only God.

8
What was Jesus saying?
2. The kingdom of God

Finding food for five thousand people out of nowhere had kicked off a big discussion among the people of Galilee. There could be no question but that something utterly marvellous had happened; there were too many witnesses around to deny it. But what did it all mean? John tells us that some people who saw the feeding of the five thousand had already decided: Jesus was going to become king of the Jews, and they were ready to make it happen by force if necessary (John 6:14–15).

Deconstructing Jesus

The great Chinese revolutionary Mao Zedong once wrote, 'Political power grows out of the barrel of a gun.' He was right, up to a point. But even revolutionaries need to eat, and you could say that lasting political power comes from the back of a bread van. In the aftermath of the feeding of the five thousand, the radical elements in the crowd began to see that Jesus had political potential, and they started making plans to take advantage of it. Significantly, John's Gospel records that Jesus became aware of this, and that he distanced himself from the possibility of revolution by simply walking away and going into hiding for a while. When the crowd eventually found him, he spoke to them at length about the real meaning of his power. *'I am the bread of life,'* he said, *'He who comes to me will never go hungry, and he who believes in me will never be thirsty'* (John 6:35).

According to John, the crowd could accept neither Jesus' refusal to act on their plans, nor the things he was saying about himself. They wanted political action, but Jesus was stressing their need to come to a radical decision about following him. *'My Father's will',* he insisted, *'is that everyone who looks to the Son and believes in him shall have eternal life'* (John 6:40). At this point, a lot of people concluded that Jesus had nothing to offer them, and even some of his more committed followers deserted him.

This is so important as we try to understand Jesus today. We do not hesitate to deconstruct our heroes and reassemble them in our own image. We do the same to Jesus too. People today are still trying to hijack him for their own political or religious agenda. Marxists in South America and right-wing members of the Moral Majority in North America both claim him as their inspiration. To others he is an eastern-style guru, or a New Age spirit-guide. We feel we have a perfect right to play these games, taking the bits of Jesus we like and leaving the rest. According to John, if we're not prepared to follow the real Jesus, he would rather we walked away and forgot him altogether.

The man from Nazareth wants us listen to his own evaluation of himself. All we have to do is to look carefully at the data the Gospel writers have given us. The real Jesus is there if we look for him, though he is more complex than our crude political agendas make him out to be. In fact, the real Jesus was a much more scary character than any radical politician or suburban guru. Israel's ancient boundaries were not nearly big enough for the kingdom he had in mind. He called his project for changing the world 'the kingdom of God'.

Where is the kingdom?

There is a country called the Kingdom of Saudi Arabia, which you will find between the Red Sea and the Persian Gulf; its capital is Riyadh. I live in the United Kingdom, a small group of islands just off the coast of continental Europe; our capital is London and it sits astride the Greenwich meridian. When Jesus spoke about 'the kingdom of God', it was natural to assume that he was talking about a place somewhere on the Earth's surface, a country with borders and a capital. It was natural for the Jews to think specifically of David's ancient kingdom, with its capital on the hill of Zion, Jerusalem.

Third-millennium people like us, looking back on the first century, find it more natural to think of the kingdom of God in more or less spiritual terms. We know that Jesus could not have been so crude as to teach about a political entity, like the UK or Saudi Arabia, so 'the kingdom of God' must mean something otherworldly. Matthew's Gospel seems to reinforce this impression, because he frequently substitutes the phrase 'the kingdom of heaven' for 'the kingdom of God'. It looks as though Jesus was pushing the expectations of his Jewish friends back beyond the grave. His kingdom would arrive at the end of time, and if the oppressed peoples of the world couldn't have justice and freedom today, they could be sure of 'pie in the sky when they die'. Actually, Jesus had neither a political dream, nor an unearthly ghost-state in mind when he spoke about the kingdom of God. His vision was altogether more wonderful and much bigger than anything his hearers could imagine.

Meet the monarch

Matthew's introduction to Jesus leaves the reader in no doubt that he is a king. The long genealogy and the visiting Magi made that clear from the beginning. This explains why Jesus kept provoking people to come to a point of decision about him and to believe in him. The starting-point of his message about the kingdom was the challenge to acknowledge Jesus himself as the king.

Crucially, the kingdom Jesus talked about did not have geographical or political boundaries. When he used the phrase 'the kingdom of God' he meant anywhere on Earth or beyond where God's rule is loved and obeyed. The kingdom consisted of individuals who had recognized Jesus as their king and were prepared to live out the implications. People like that could live anywhere on the globe, not just in Judah. They did not even have to live together, though groups of them would form communities the world over. Jesus was talking not so much about a 'kingdom' as about his active 'kingly rule' over the lives of those who acknowledge him as their monarch. You might say that God's kingdom is *dynamic*. It is not about where you live, but about whether God is actively ruling in your life.

It is difficult to get the feel of what Jesus taught about the kingdom from the bare description I am trying to give you now. Whenever Jesus wanted to describe an aspect of the kingdom, he told a story about it. His parables engage our imagination and invite us to work things out for ourselves. Matthew grouped seven of Jesus' parables about the kingdom of God in chapter 13 of his Gospel. These are the best guide to Jesus' kingdom project, so it makes sense to look at them closely.

Stories with a meaning

The parables of Jesus are stories with a meaning. They are mostly about farming and fishing, though some involve scenes from the lives of managers and merchants. They have one thing in common: though they are set in the first-century world, they are all easily accessible in any culture or any time. Anyone who has ever watered a plant, kept a goldfish or lusted after an expensive bauble behind a shop window will be able to understand most of the parables fairly quickly. At least, that is what you would think, but Jesus did occasionally use these stories to conceal his meaning rather than to reveal it. It is as though he wanted his hearers to pester him about what he meant. As we shall see, this happens in the case of the first story we are going to look at.

Here's an example from Matthew's collection, the first of his seven parables of the kingdom:

> *A farmer went out to sow his seed. As he was scattering the seed, some fell along the path, and the birds came and ate it up. Some fell on rocky places, where it did not have much soil. It sprang up quickly, because the soil was shallow. But when the sun came up, the plants were scorched, and they withered because they had no root. Other seed fell among thorns, which grew up and choked the plants. Still other seed fell on good soil,*

where it produced a crop ... a hundred, sixty or thirty
times what was sown. He who has ears, let him hear
(Matthew 13:3–9).

The story is easy to picture, but what does it mean?
Jesus said that we must get our ears in tune with the
message of the parables: '*He who has ears, let him hear.*' His
friends were baffled when they first heard him speaking
like this, and waited until they were alone with him before
asking what on earth it was about. At first, he spoke
mysteriously, as if the stories were meant to conceal the
truth; but he sooon explained the story so that they would
learn how to interpret his picture-language:

Listen then to what the parable of the sower means:
When anyone hears the message about the kingdom
and does not understand it, the evil one comes and
snatches away what was sown in his heart. This is
the seed sown along the path. The one who received the
seed that fell on rocky places is the man who hears
the word and at once receives it with joy. But since he
has no root, he lasts only a short time. When trouble or
persecution comes because of the word, he quickly falls
away. The one who received the seed that fell among
the thorns is the man who hears the word, but the
worries of this life and the deceitfulness of wealth choke
it, making it unfruitful. But the one who received the
seed that fell on good soil is the man who hears the
word and understands it. He produces a crop, yielding
a hundred, sixty or thirty times what was sown
(Matthew 13:18–23).

The meaning is not difficult to grasp. The kingdom
grows in influence as people hear about it and accept what

they have heard. The kingdom's impact on an individual will vary because a person's allegiance to it is tested by the circumstances of life. The aim is to be as productive as possible. There's one other thing: the kingdom makes no impact at all on those who cannot be bothered to try to understand it, whereas the one who takes the trouble to understand is the one who becomes most productive.

There is a lot of detail in Jesus' explanation of this parable, and most of his stories are much simpler than this. Even so, one simple fact sticks out of this story: a personal response to the message about the kingdom is absolutely essential. Are you in or are you out? If you are in, how much impact will the words of the king make in your life?

The second parable in Matthew's sequence is another picture drawn from farming. Here a field is planted by a farmer but sown with weeds by an enemy (Matthew 13:24–30). Once more the disciples needed help to tune into Jesus message.

The one who sowed the good seed is the Son of Man. The field is the world, and the good seed stands for the sons of the kingdom. The weeds are the sons of the evil one, and the enemy who sows them is the devil. The harvest is the end of the age, and the harvesters are angels.

As the weeds are pulled up and burned in the fire, so it will be at the end of the age. The Son of Man will send out his angels, and they will weed out of his kingdom everything that causes sin and all who do evil. They will throw them into the fiery furnace, where there will be weeping and gnashing of teeth. Then the righteous will shine like the sun in the kingdom of their Father. He who has ears, let him hear (Matthew 13:37–43).

Now this is altogether more serious. Jesus himself is the one who is scattering the message about the kingdom; he is building a community of those who recognize him as king. Yet they have an enemy, for the evil one is also sowing his message and recruiting a following. At the end of time there will be a terrible judgment and the children of the kingdom will be separated from the children of darkness. Those who have committed themselves to God's way of living will enjoy his blessing for ever, but those who serve the evil one will face a dreadful punishment. Only two ways to live are on offer, and you must choose; your destiny will be shaped by the decision you make.

Personal loyalty, public impact

So far, it looks as though the kingdom of God is about a personal response to the teaching of Jesus. Two more of Jesus' pictures show how he expected his disciples' decisions to influence the world:

> *The kingdom of heaven is like a mustard seed, which a man took and planted in his field. Though it is the smallest of all your seeds, yet when it grows, it is the largest of garden plants and becomes a tree, so that the birds of the air come and perch in its branches.*
> *… the kingdom of heaven is like yeast that a woman took and mixed into a large amount of flour until it worked all through the dough* (Matthew 13:31–33).

Both these pictures make a similar point: the kingdom has small beginnings but great influence. The tiny mustard seed becomes the biggest bush in the herb garden and a shelter for the garden birds trying to avoid the claws of the village cat. In the same way, the community of the king will become a shelter from the storm for those who need it. The lump of yeast makes a large amount of dough rise, and the people of the king have the task of influencing the whole of society.

Being part of the kingdom of God is not a private religious affair. The citizens of the kingdom have an interest in the world around them, to give shelter to the fragile and to spread the influence of the king as far as it will go. Simple pictures make the message clear: the community of the king will seek to influence society for good, and to give shelter to its victims.

Because he's worth it!

Jesus often spoke about the need to look for the kingdom. It is as though something of infinite value exists right under our noses and we don't realize it. Two little stories develop this theme:

> *The kingdom of heaven is like treasure hidden in a field. When a man found it, he hid it again, and then in his joy went and sold all he had and bought that field.*
>
> *Again, the kingdom of heaven is like a merchant looking for fine pearls. When he found one of great value, he went away and sold everything he had and bought it* (Matthew 13:44–46).

The search is worth it because the treasure is worth finding. The hired worker in the field hits the loot with his shovel and within minutes is off to sell everything he has to buy the land, because it is worth it. You can see him in you mind's eye, nonchalantly negotiating the price and trying not to look too excited when the owner agrees to sell. The wealthy merchant, who has been looking at fine pearls all his life, is examining the latest arrivals on a boat from the mystic East when his jaw drops to the floor. In front of him is a pearl the like of which he has never seen before. The cool businessman quietly pops it back into its bag, and goes home to put every possession he has on the market, because it is worth it.

Peter and his friends had gradually realized that Jesus was the promised Messiah. Others were still struggling to work out what the clues meant. Jesus himself did not often say publicly, 'I am the Messiah', because he would have been widely misunderstood as initiating a political restoration of Israel. Jesus' project was quite different. He spoke with authority, acted with power, and encouraged people to work out who he really was for themselves. 'This is a treasure hunt,' these parables are saying. Jesus himself is the treasure in the field and the pearl on board the boat. It is not just twenty-first-century people who puzzle over him; they did so then, too. Once more, the message in the picture is simple: Jesus' kingdom is worth all the effort you put into finding the truth, and everything it may cost you to become part of the project.

Past, present and future

The plan to bring God's reign into the lives of human beings began with the personal arrival of the king himself. You could say that God's kingdom has already come with the advent of Jesus. Yet each of these parables gives us a sense of a reign which is growing in influence as people respond one by one to the message of the king. Its growth is resisted by the pressures of persecution or materialism, or by the activities of the evil one. As the influence of the kingdom grows, the communities that represent it on earth influence society and shelter the vulnerable. The kingdom has come, and it is still growing; but there will come a time when it will arrive in awesome fullness and sweep away all opposition.

This brings us to the final story in Matthew's septet. It looks into the future, to the moment, hinted at already, when the end of time arrives and a final revolution takes place.

> *Once again, the kingdom of heaven is like a net that was let down into the lake and caught all kinds of fish. When it was full, the fishermen pulled it up on the shore. Then they sat down and collected the good fish in baskets, but threw the bad away. This is how it will be at the end of the age. The angels will come and separate the wicked from the righteous and throw them into the fiery furnace, where there will be weeping and gnashing of teeth* (Matthew 13:47–50).

This terrifying picture takes us to the final judgment of the human race, promised by the kingdom. There is no missing the simple point of this picture: the reign of God will one day be expressed in the separation of humanity and in the punishment of the wicked.

This raises a difficult issue for twenty-first-century people who have deconstructed the real Jesus. He has been recast as an anaemic figure who would never allow anyone to face the kind of judgment this parable describes. It is true that Jesus frequently sided with the people his society had abandoned, and that his kingdom project brought the possibility of new life and direction for them. He wanted everyone to be part of it. Yet it was Jesus himself who insisted that the climax of the project would be a worldwide judgment, and he spoke openly about the terrible consequences of rejecting him and his kingdom. The kingdom is coming in all its awesome fullness, he insisted; nothing can stop it.

There is a solemn moment at the climax of Handel's great oratorio *Messiah* when the chorus sings: 'The kingdom of this world is become the kingdom of our Lord and of his Christ, and he shall reign for ever and ever.' The words are taken from the Revelation to John (11:15), the last book of the New Testament, and describe the time when a new humanity is given a new start in a new heaven and a new earth. This is how Jesus saw the future too: the triumph of the kingdom over the forces that tried to extinguish it, and the ultimate victory of good over evil.

Jesus' vision of the kingdom of God was bigger than the Jewish agenda, and more down to earth than our twenty-first-century ideas. It was a plan that centred on him personally, and demanded that people come to a decision about his status in their lives.

But getting his contemporaries to see that the kingdom of God was coming through his ministry was a tough job. The old ideas had an iron grip on people's minds. This was brought home powerfully one day when John the Baptist sent some of his team to talk with Jesus. It must have been a disturbing moment; his longest-standing and highest-profile supporter now had serious doubts.

9
Training the team

John was disturbed by the slow arrival of God's judgment, and sent a team of his followers to find out the reason for the delay. Jesus sent the message back that his ministry was bursting with signs that the power of God was being unleashed in acts of mercy and love. *'Go back and report to John what you hear and see'*, he said to the messengers. *'The blind receive sight, the lame walk, those who have leprosy are cured ...'* (Matthew 11:4–5). The kingdom would bring judgment, but Jesus was preparing for a long interlude when God's forgiveness and mercy would be offered to humanity. Essential to this strategy was the training of an effective team to do the job.

Apostles: accredited messengers

As we saw in chapter 5, it was natural for a distinguished rabbi to gather a group of disciples around him. They would soak up his teaching in the hope that they too

121

would become rabbis one day. Jesus took this accepted practice a step further. For a start, he was constantly on the move, and he needed a group of people who would go with him wherever he went and suffer the same privations. Other rabbis did not travel as much, and tended to wait for potential pupils to come to them. Moreover, he was not calling his friends into a life of academic study. His intention was to equip a group of people who could increase the impact of his ministry in Galilee, and then take over from him altogether.

As the crowds around Jesus ebbed and flowed, he hand-picked a group of men to form the inner core of his team. They were *disciples*, in that they had a serious commitment to following Jesus, but he gave twelve of them the new title *apostles*, which set them apart from the others. Their title pointed up their future role; an apostle was a commissioned representative having the authority of the person who sent him. These men were preparing to be the leaders of the movement Jesus founded, that would one day become known as the church. The number was probably significant, too. Ancient Israel had been made up of twelve tribes, and choosing twelve apostles may have been a symbolic move to illustrate the renewing of Israel that was part of Jesus' mission. The number was certainly important to the twelve themselves, for when one of them betrayed Jesus and committed suicide they felt the need to appoint a replacement. The criterion they would use to choose a new member of the twelve is interesting: *'it is necessary to choose one of the men who have been with us the whole time the Lord Jesus went in and out among us, beginning from John's baptism to the time when Jesus was taken up from us. For one of these must become a witness with us of his resurrection'* (Acts 1:21–22).

This fascinating passage tells us two things. First, each

of the twelve had followed Jesus from early on in his ministry, so they were able to bear witness to all his activities. Secondly, there were other disciples, not included in the twelve, who had followed Jesus consistently through this whole period. Matthias (who was chosen to fill the gap) was one of these, but there were many others. At one time, there were at least seventy-two committed disciples working with Jesus in the Galilee area (Luke 10:1). Besides the twelve personally commissioned by Jesus, some individuals were later designated apostles by the early churches.

(There's no getting away from the fact that Jesus chose twelve *men*. The Gospels are most unusual among ancient literature, however, in the prominence they give to women. Later, in the first Christian communities, some women occupied leadership roles. There is even a hint that a woman apostle was working in the different cultural atmosphere of Rome [Romans 16:7; Junias was a woman's name] though this is a disputed point.)

The A team

Bearing in mind the crucial importance of each team member, it is worth looking at the mix of people that Jesus deliberately put together. His first choices were moderately prosperous businessmen, the Galilean fishermen and brothers Simon Peter and Andrew. The extrovert Simon seems to have pushed Andrew into the background a little. Andrew worked behind the scenes, while Simon and the brothers James and John became an inner group that Jesus seems to have regarded as especially close to him.

Matthew (Levi) came in early too. He was certainly not poor, and as a tax collector he would be educated and multilingual. Roman officials would have regarded him as a notable citizen of Galilee and accorded him a level of respect above the rest of the population. Yet Jews would have seen him as a Roman collaborator, and as ceremonially unclean because he had contact with Gentiles. Jesus also drew into the twelve a man called Simon 'the Zealot'. The Zealots were hard-line nationalists who hated everything to do with Rome; some of them were pretty violent. Levi and Simon were two men with a lot to fight about!

Whatever fights they had along the way (and the Gospels admit they had a few), the team grew close together. Several of them had affectionate nicknames; for example, Thomas was called 'Didymus', or 'the twin', and he seems to have been a natural sceptic. James and John were dubbed 'the Sons of Thunder'. One wonders if they had problems with their digestion, but it seems more likely that they shared a fiery temperament; there are several examples of their short-tempered and ambitious nature in the Gospels. The most famous nickname of all is that of Simon, whose Hebrew surname was Cephas. In Greek, this translated into Petros, the word for a stone or small rock. We call him Peter, and there's a rather large building named after him in Rome. Simon Peter is always named first whenever the Gospel writers list the apostles, and he often appears as the spokesman of the team. He was a gigantic figure in the early church.

It is likely that John was the youngest disciple. A Christian leader in Ephesus, writing in about AD 190, says that John died there during the reign of the Roman emperor Trajan (between AD 98 and 117). This would put his death at around AD 100. Jesus was crucified around AD 29, so John was probably still in his teens when he and his brother James left their fishing business to go on the road with Jesus. If this is the case, the others were not much older. Jesus himself was in his early thirties, and most of his team would lead a vigorous, active life for many years to come. Peter was crucified during a vicious persecution of Christians in Rome in the years AD 64 to 65 (that is, up to thirty-eight years after he became a disciple). He may have been around the same age as Jesus when they first met. Compared with some modern church leaders, the A team was a youth movement.

People sometimes imagine that Jesus' friends were highly disreputable low life pulled out of the gutters of Galilee. Everything we know about them tells us this was not the case. For a start, they would not have been uneducated. Hundreds of archaeological finds demonstrate that many ordinary people could read and write. Four languages were in daily use in Galilee. Aramaic was the language of the streets, and Hebrew the language of the synagogues. Greek was the common language throughout the empire, and Latin was the language of the Romans. Between them, the apostles could communicate effectively in all four. Most of his followers were not from poor families; some were even well to do, like the three women mentioned by Luke (8:1–3). They were not, however, the kind of people to have been accepted by the existing religious groups such as the Pharisees or the Essenes. In choosing his twelve apostles Jesus was sending a message: his kingdom was inclusive, and not the preserve of a religious elite.

Elite they were not! A breathtaking fact about the apostles is the warts-and-all way they are presented in the Gospels. Considering the status of these men by the time the Gospels were written, you would have thought that the writers would have been keen to hide their early blunders. Yet few of the apostles escape looking foolish or cowardly. At first, they are swept along by the tide of events, but, as Jesus introduces them to his real agenda, they either fail to understand what he is talking about or oppose him altogether. Simon Peter, the one who would become more prominent than most of them, is given the harshest treatment of them all by Matthew:

From that time on Jesus began to explain to his disciples that he must go to Jerusalem and suffer many things at the hands of the elders, chief priests and teachers of the law, and that he must be killed and on the third day be raised to life.

Peter took him aside and began to rebuke him. 'Never, Lord!' he said. 'This shall never happen to you!'

Jesus turned and said to Peter, 'Get behind me, Satan! You are a stumbling-block to me; you do not have in mind the things of God, but the things of men' (Matthew 16:21–23).

The write-up they get does not improve from here. Simon Peter consistently fails to comprehend Jesus' mission. Eventually, he denies knowing him, and abandons him altogether. Mark, whose main source was Peter himself, presents all this in an equally harsh light. It is evidence of the integrity of the apostles that they resisted the urge to suppress this kind of material when they passed on their memories of their time with Jesus.

The other apostles do not get a better press. They are caught arguing about which of them is the greatest, and James and John try to outflank the others by getting their mother to lobby Jesus to give them the best seats in the kingdom of heaven.

One thing is obvious from this: Jesus had more faith in these men than they had in Jesus. His strategy with them involved a programme of intensive training that began the moment they left their day jobs behind to follow him.

Teaching men to change the world

From the start, they were watching Jesus in action and listening to him teach. We know that they will also have been memorizing Jesus' teaching, because that was the usual way in which a disciple learnt his master's words in order to pass them on. Most of Jesus' teaching was presented in the traditional semi-poetic form beloved of ancient rabbis. This was designed to make it easy to memorize. If you want to check this out, think back to the last chapter of this book. Now jot down an outline of the parable of the sower. You will find that most of it comes to mind fairly easily, although you have not yet made any attempt to memorize it. Look at the story itself in Matthew 13:3–8, and you will see an obvious structure. It wouldn't take you long to commit this passage to memory.

Soon the team was being asked to do more than to listen to Jesus' words; they were pushed out into Galilee to reproduce Jesus' works. Matthew builds up a picture of the growing authority of Jesus as he acts with power in the sequence of stories in chapters 8 and 9 of his Gospel. In chapter 10 there is a significant development: *'He called his twelve disciples to him and gave them authority to drive out evil spirits and to heal every disease and sickness.'* (verse 1). Then he sent them out into the towns and villages of Galilee to preach, heal and cast out demons.

This training exercise was a foretaste of their future ministry. For the moment, they had to concentrate on one ethnic group, and, to make it easy for them, it was their own race, the Jews. Nevertheless, it was a challenge. They were to carry a minimum of provisions and no money, relying on God to look after their needs. They were to set out to do some of the things Jesus had done: *' As you go, preach this message: "The kingdom of heaven is near." Heal*

*the sick, raise the dead, cleanse those who have leprosy, drive
out demons. Freely you have received, freely give'* (verses 7–8).

Some of Jesus' authority had passed to them, and their
mission was a complete success. Yet they returned
exhausted and desperate for rest. It was then that they
couldn't escape the crowds, and, as Mark describes it, the
sequence of events that led to the feeding of the five
thousand was set in motion.

As the huge crowd trailed, sheep-like, after Jesus into
the wilderness, and as it became obvious that they needed
food, Jesus turned to his trainees and challenged them:
'You give them something to eat' (Mark 6:37). It seems
absurd to us, as though Jesus was trying to humiliate his
friends. Of course, they were at a loss, and passed the
problem back to their master. But Jesus' challenge was
serious, even if it was spoken with a twinkle in his eye;
after the mission to Galilee they had crossed the threshold
from being spectators to being players. They had the
authority; now they needed the faith and experience to
know what to do in each situation.

These were skills that proved difficult to master. On
one occasion, when Jesus was absent, some of his team
were approached by a man whose son was suffering from
demon possession. The poor man was distraught and desperate for help. The disciples waded in, and found to their
horror that their best efforts could not liberate the boy. It
does not take much to imagine the effect this had on the
father, who intercepted Jesus on his way back to rejoin his
friends. The man begged for help. Within a few minutes
the mess was sorted out and the boy was well again.

His disciples were confused. Their technique had
worked before; why didn't it work now? Jesus' reply has
become famous: *'Because you have so little faith. I tell you
the truth, if you have faith as small as a mustard seed, you*

can say to this mountain, "Move from here to there" and it will move. Nothing will be impossible for you' (Matthew 17:20).

The disciples were not just learning facts about the kingdom; they were developing skills in acts of faith that would show the power of the kingdom to their hearers. Jesus worked in words and wonders and, though many of his miracles were unique and unrepeatable, the apostles would have to repeat some of them if they were to have the required impact.

Radical leadership

In our twenty-first-century world we are very conscious of status. Someone who drives a BMW has 'arrived', but if you drive a Lada you have reached the wrong destination altogether. I have actually seen grown men weep with shame because they have had to exchange their prestige car for something they think is beneath them. Human beings are status addicts. So it is not surprising that the disciples were interested in status too. Some of them were ambitious, and wanted to be seen as greater than the others. All of them got a serious shock as Jesus began to live out his ideas about status.

'Who is the greatest in the kingdom of heaven?' they asked one day (Matthew 18:1). Jesus got a child to stand up in front of them. Children had no status in first-century Palestine, and little legal protection. They were society's most vulnerable members. *'Whoever humbles himself like this child is the greatest in the kingdom of heaven'* Jesus said (verse 4). Everything he said about status was upside down as far as the rest of the world was concerned. He expected his disciples to see things from his point of view, even if they had to stand on their heads to do it.

This became central to everything he taught them about leadership. The leadership style of the religious and political establishment was exactly the reverse of Jesus' ideals for the kingdom:

> *You know that the rulers of the Gentiles lord it over them, and their high officials exercise authority over them. Not so with you. Instead, whoever wants to become great among you must be your servant, and whoever wants to be first must be your slave – just as the Son of Man did not come to be served, but to serve, and to give his life as a ransom for many* (Matthew 20:25–28).

Servant leadership was more than a theory; it was Jesus' lifestyle. If he really was the Son of Man, he could claim higher status than anyone. But instead he came to serve, and give his life.

Much later, on the eve of his trial and death, he left his friends with a vivid picture of this servant attitude, which only John records (13:1–17). As they gathered for their annual Passover meal, they came in from the dusty street and sat round the table, looking forward to the feast. It was customary for a household slave to wash the dirt off the guests' feet before they went in to eat, but, there being no such person present, the disciples had to do without that formality. Maybe a frisson of embarrassment was going round the room. If no slave was available to do this job, another lowly person would usually do it; but on this occasion nobody made a move. Clearly, the work was beneath any of those present.

It was not beneath Jesus' dignity, however. Getting up from the table and taking off his outer robe, he picked up a bowl and a towel and began to wash the disciples' feet himself. Kneeling in front of each one, the leader of the team did the job of the lowest slave in the pecking order. Simon Peter was so appalled by what Jesus was doing that he would not let his feet be touched. But Jesus quietly insisted, and Simon gave in.

Having finished, Jesus sat down and summed up the lesson of the incident:

> *You call me 'Teacher' and 'Lord', and rightly so, for that is what I am. Now that I, your Lord and Teacher, have washed your feet, you also should wash one another's feet. I have set you an example that you should do as I have done for you. I tell you the truth, no servant is greater than his master, nor is a messenger greater than the one who sent him. Now that you know these things, you will be blessed if you do them* (John 13:13–17).

Last Christmas I went to a local department store to buy presents. Near the entrance was a shoeshine stand, a chair with a place to put your feet while a man cleaned and polished your shoes. I stopped for a while and watched, trying to imagine how I would feel if I had to do that job in that place, squatting on the floor in front of everyone and cleaning someone else's shoes. I supposed I would do it if that was the only way I could earn money to feed my family, but I recoiled at the thought.

'Shoeshine boy' – that is what Jesus was for his disciples that night. The kind of behaviour he modelled should be normal for those who aspire to leadership in his kingdom project.

Lives on the line

Servant leadership was not the only lesson the disciples had to struggle with. While all this was happening, the team received some bad news. John the Baptist had been beheaded on the orders of Herod Antipas. Mark's account of the events leading up to the execution looks as though it had escaped from the pages of the *Arabian Nights* (see Mark 6:17–29).

Although Herod had had John arrested (we met this story in chapter 4), he had a superstitious reluctance to hurt John because of the righteous atmosphere that surrounded him. Herod's wife Herodias, by contrast, wanted him dead. So John stayed put in the basement of the fortress. Things would have stayed this way if Herod had not thrown a party for his friends on his birthday. It was an all-male affair, but Herodias' daughter was the cabaret, performing a sensual dance so pleasing to the guests that Herod felt he ought to make a grand gesture to reward her. He must have been well drunk.

'Ask me for anything you want, and I'll give it to you,' he promised. *'Whatever you ask I will give you, up to half my kingdom'.*

The girl went and consulted her mother about this once-in-a-lifetime offer. Herodias didn't hesitate: 'Ask for the head of John the Baptist,' she said.

The dancer ran back to the party and approached the tetrarch with her mother's request, adding a few embellishments of her own: *'Give me right now the head of John the Baptist on a platter.'*

Herod was upset, but could not back down. John was doomed.

The news was a forewarning of things to come. The disciples were now aware that people who announce a kingdom of righteousness must expect the world to react violently. Some of Jesus' team would one day pay a similar price. Peter eventually reached Rome and helped to nurture the Christian community there. He was executed under Nero. According to tradition, he was crucified upside down outside the city walls. John lived into his nineties and died in Ephesus. For many years he had been held on the prison island of Patmos, the Alcatraz of the Roman world. His brother James had died long before, executed by Herod Agrippa around AD 44. Andrew is thought to have been crucified somewhere in southern Greece. One tradition about Thomas says that he found his way to the south of India, where he founded a Christian community that survives to this day, before he too was killed.

The fate of Jesus' other friends, as they fanned out across the known world, is lost in antiquity. Wherever they went they talked about Jesus, demonstrated his power to heal and to deliver people, planted Christian communities and moved on. Some of them died in such obscurity that no reliable tradition survives regarding their fate. Yet, by the time the last of them died, there were well over half a million followers of Jesus in the Mediterranean world. Jesus had trained his people well.

10

What was Jesus like?

When I was a teenager I took my girlfriend to see the musical *Jesus Christ Superstar*. I left the theatre puzzled. How could a wimp like that, who couldn't have punched his way out of a wet paper bag, have made such a deep impact on the world? I shared my theological question with my date, whose reply stunned me. 'Don't say that!' she exclaimed. 'He looked lovely!'

The *Superstar* Jesus repelled me because he seemed so weak, but my friend was drawn to him because he looked nice. I realized then that her taste in men didn't correspond with my idea of manhood, and with a sinking feeling I saw that our relationship was doomed.

What did Jesus look like, and what kind of a man was he? Over the centuries, great artists have tried to answer that question. As a result, we all have a picture of Jesus in our heads, derived from a movie, a painting or even a sculpture.

What did Jesus look like?

A beautiful sculpture from the Museo de Terme in Rome is one of the earliest. It dates from around AD 350 and has Jesus sitting in the posture of a teacher. He is clean-shaven, dressed in a flowing toga, and has short, curly hair. There was no doubt in the unknown sculptor's mind that Jesus looked just like an Italian. Yet the images of Jesus in Byzantine art, with his long, dark hair and carefully shaped beard, make him look exactly like a nobleman from Constantinople at the turn of the eleventh century. Most striking of all is Salvador Dali's *The Crucifixion*. Here Jesus hangs on a cross, suspended over planet Earth. It puts Jesus in an imaginary space between fantasy and reality. This is a very twentieth-century Jesus. Is he real? Who knows?

How odd it seems to us that the Gospels do not devote a single word to describing Jesus' appearance! Yet it was a typical omission for the period; biographical works of the first century hardly ever gave the kind of information that we today crave. In the absence of hard information, every age has tended to visualize Jesus in its own image: a Roman teacher, a Byzantine noble or a weirdo. This is not completely unhelpful, since if Jesus was physically living among us today, he would be dressed like one of us, not like a character out of a nativity play.

The Gospels leave the question of Jesus' appearance out of the frame. What matters are his actions and words. Whatever I imagine Jesus looked like, I must answer the questions: how would he be different from me? What was it like to spend time with him? What kind of person was he? Would I find myself drawn to him or not? Was he a man or a mouse? What impact did his personality make on those around him? It is not difficult to find answers to the important questions from the material we have available.

The real Jesus

Jesus was a truly remarkable individual. It is common knowledge that he was tender-hearted with those on the periphery of society, and that he went out of his way to bring healing and a sense of significance to people few others cared about. It is not often appreciated that he was also capable of vigorous aggression when he felt the truth was under attack. He was no pushover, but defied the *status quo* and demanded to be heard. The doe-eyed Jesus of sentimental imagination, 'gentle Jesus, meek and mild', never existed. The real man was tough as well as tender, sensitive to the feelings of the vulnerable and yet possessing an incisive intelligence that would not tolerate religious humbug or dishonesty.

On top of this, he was powerful, repeatedly demonstrating his ability to command the forces of nature. Power like that could have won him the things that most men want, yet he didn't want them. Power did not corrupt this astonishing man as he lived by the principle that to lead is to serve others. And yet he kept making almost megalomaniac claims about himself. When you add them all up, they amount to a claim to divinity. He never actually said, 'I am God', but his words and actions left the disciples no option but to come to this conclusion. From the earliest times, Christian communities have worshipped Jesus as God incarnate. You cannot get more remarkable than that.

Controversy: Jesus fights his corner

First-century Galilee and Judea were unstable places. A

fiercely nationalistic people was ruled by an uncompromisingly brutal empire. It was an explosive mixture that eventually went critical in AD 70 with a tragic and bloody rebellion. In this atmosphere, a careless word could cost you your life, and a conspicuous celebrity like Jesus could be asked some tough questions. Mark records a breathtaking question-and-answer session with Jesus under fire from a group of Pharisees and Sadducees (Mark 12:13–34). He makes it clear that Jesus began the trouble with a sharply pointed parable aimed at exposing the failures of this very group of people. They did not take the criticism lying down, but weighed in with question after question.

'Do you think we ought to pay taxes to Caesar, or not?' a Pharisee asked him. Immediately, people's ears pricked up. The Roman sympathizers and agents would be on the lookout for rebellion, and the Jewish nationalists would be listening for a rallying cry against their oppressors. Anything Jesus said could cause a crisis and might even lead to bloodshed. At times like this, politicians resort to bland phrases that mean nothing. But Jesus didn't.

'Show me a coin,' he said. Someone produced a small one-denarius piece and handed it to him. Holding the coin up, he asked them, 'Whose image can you see on the coin?' It was like the build-up to a magic trick. Was he going to make the thing disappear up his sleeve?

Someone in the group chirped up, 'It's the image of Caesar.'

'That's right', Jesus said. 'So give Caesar what belongs to him, and give to God what belongs to him.'

It was a clever way of affirming the right of the ruler to levy taxes while giving a message only Jewish people would understand. The ancient Scriptures said that human beings were made in the image of God; every person had

God's image stamped on him or her in the same way that the coin bore Caesar's image. To those in the know, Jesus' words affirmed that you could honour both the imperial ruler and God, if you gave them both what belonged to them. Jesus could think on his feet.

The Sadducees weighed in next, probing the technical weaknesses of Jesus' teaching with obscure theological questions. Jesus refused to play the game. 'Do you know what your problem is?' he asked. 'You have no idea how powerful God really is!' In a few sentences he demolished the arrogant and aristocratic Sadducees, leaving them looking foolish.

A fully qualified teacher of the law happened to be passing at that moment, and was so impressed with the way Jesus fielded questions that he decided to lob in one of his own. *'Of all the commandments, which is the most important?'*

This needed a careful answer. The law of God was contained in five sacred books and there were hundreds of detailed regulations. Jesus' reply has become famous: *'The most important one … is this: "Hear O Israel, the Lord our God, the Lord is one. Love the Lord your God with all your heart and with all your soul and with all your mind and with all your strength." The second is this: "Love your neighbour as yourself." There is no commandment greater than these.'*

The accredited teacher of the law was impressed by the answer given by the untrained carpenter, and said as much. In the middle of an intellectual fist-fight, Jesus warmed to the man. *'You are not far from the kingdom of God,'* he said.

There is a difference between a genuine question and a combative one designed to keep the truth at a distance. Jesus had deep respect for people who had a genuine passion for the truth. Intelligent people are often insensitive to the feelings of those who do not share their superior abilities. You would expect a man of Jesus' sharpness to be a little hard, and distant from the rest of us. Was that the case?

Sensitivity: individuals matter

Now and then I read a passage of the Gospels and wonder what on earth is going on. A prime example is the story of the healing of a deaf and dumb man told by Mark (7:31–37). A crowd of people approached Jesus as he was returning from a trip into Gentile country around the city of Tyre in what we now call the Lebanon. One of them was the deaf and dumb man, who was led along by some of his friends. Jesus was renowned for his healing ability; he could heal by touch or even at a distance by saying the word. But when he met this individual, he did something entirely different. He led the man away from the crowd, who watched as Jesus put his fingers in the man's ears, spat on to the ground, touched the man's tongue and then began to speak. It seems a strange routine for Jesus to go through.

I once shared my incomprehension of this story with a friend who works with deaf children. Her insight was enlightening. First, Sue took me through the actual words Mark uses, because I had got them wrong. 'Mark says the man was *deaf and could hardly talk*,' she told me. 'This is exactly right. The man wasn't dumb at all; he just hadn't learned to speak properly because he couldn't hear other people making the sounds.' Mark had described a common medical condition and I had missed it! 'A deaf person like this would not know what was happening, and the crowd would scare him half to death,' Sue went on.

'His friends asked Jesus to put his hands on him, but this was likely to scare him even more.'

I imagined being unable to hear and having someone come towards me with both hands stretched out. Would this stranger heal me or strangle me? I could see the point.

'So Jesus had the sensitivity to take the man far enough away from the crowd to be able to communicate with him,' Sue said.

I wondered how you would communicate with a deaf man who doesn't know sign language. Then it struck me: 'Jesus made up a sign language. He put his fingers in the man's ears and touched his tongue.'

'That's right,' Sue said. 'And he spoke to the man, because it was possible he could lip-read a little. A lot of deaf people can.'

I was excited by this; something I had never really understood was becoming clear. 'Did you notice that Mark records the actual word Jesus spoke to the man?' Sue asked.

I hadn't. There are some significant points in the Gospels at which something Jesus said is written first in his own language of Aramaic, then translated. This was one of those times. 'He said, *"Ephphatha!"*, an Aramaic word that means *"Be opened!"*'

Sue smiled. 'Say the word out loud,' she said.

I had a go. 'Eff-fa-tha!' The penny dropped. 'That must have been the easiest word to lip-read in the Aramaic language!'

Jesus was no remote intellectual. He could get into the heads of others and feel their limitations, and he would adjust his own approach to suit them. His style was so different from that of the mass culture we are trained to accept. He loved and respected individuals and, though people came to him in large numbers, each received something different. Trace the stories in the Gospels of those who met Jesus, and you'll see that no two people are dealt with in the same way.

The man at the centre of the gospel story is quite unlike anyone else – tough and tender, sensitive and intelligent. He was a leader without arrogance, powerful without being corrupted. Everyone he met was changed in some way by the encounter. You could be persuaded or repelled by him, but you could not remain neutral. He was able to accept the worst of people, and help them to feel his acceptance. At the same time, he would not accept the worst *in* people, but set out to challenge and change it.

Drawing near to the city

As Jesus' wider travelling ministry drew to a close, he began to repeat his prediction that he would be betrayed and crucified. All four Gospels describe his arrival in Jerusalem in time to celebrate the Passover with his friends. What would it have been like to have met Jesus during these last few weeks of his life? As I try to give you the feel of this, I need your help. I want to use part of John's Gospel (chapter 12) to make the scene as authentic as I can. You must imagine that you have come to Jerusalem to celebrate the great annual feast of Passover. Though you know a bit of Hebrew, you cannot speak the everyday language of Judea, which is Aramaic.

This is a wonderful event for you. Generations of your family have lived in Greece but held on to their Jewish identity, and now you have made the journey to find your spiritual roots. As the city comes into sight, it looks bigger and more magnificent than anything you have ever seen before. Someone in the group begins to sing: *'That is where the tribes go up, the tribes of the LORD, to praise the name of the LORD.'* They are chanting the ancient pilgrim-song for the arrival at the gate of Jerusalem. You join in: *'Pray for the peace of Jerusalem: "May those who love you be secure. May there be peace within your walls ... "'* (Psalm 122:4, 6). This is indeed a mighty city, as beautiful to look at as any in Greece or Asia Minor, and it is teeming with people all arriving for the feast.

As you enter the city gates, you hear the crowds on the road behind you burst into song – not your song, but another: *'Hosannah!'* they are shouting. *'Hosannah! Blessed is he who comes in the name of the Lord!'* (Mark 11:9). Another procession is making its way towards the city, and people are waving palm branches and throwing them on to the road. At the head of it is a man riding on a donkey. It all strikes you as rather exotic and wonderful, and when someone gives you a palm branch you join in and shout with the crowd too.

There's a man in a doorway watching the fun, and you ask him who is leading the procession.

'He is Jesus of Nazareth,' he shouts at you. 'Some think he is the Messiah, and others think he is a charlatan, but me – I can't be bothered!'

Later, you discover that Jesus is in trouble with the authorities for his attitudes to Jewish tradition, and there is a rumour that a wealthy man from Bethany died a few days ago and Jesus brought him back to life. This bothers you, and so you try to find where Jesus is staying and see what you can discover for yourself.

Jesus and his followers have occupied a corner of the temple precincts and, as you arrive, two men notice you and introduce themselves. Their names are Andrew and Philip, and they confirm that they have seen Jesus raise people from the dead and do many other things besides. You ask them if it might be possible to speak to Jesus yourself.

The man you meet is dressed very much like any other man, and there is little to distinguish him physically from the others in the group. He holds out his hand to greet you, and you see that he must have earned a living with these hands for most of his life, for they are big and powerful, hard and callused. But he is warm and friendly, though he seems tired; and as he speaks the atmosphere becomes a little morbid. Andrew speaks your language, and translates as Jesus speaks:

'Now my heart is troubled, and what shall I say? "Father, save me from this hour"? No, it was for this very reason I came to this hour. Father, glorify your name.' (John 12 :27).

It all seems very gloomy. 'What is he talking about, Andrew?' you ask.

'He has been convinced for a year or so now that he will be betrayed and killed in Jerusalem,' Andrew replies. 'He feels that this is the time, and he wants to celebrate one last Passover with us before he dies.'

As Jesus speaks, some of Jesus' followers translate his words for the benefit of people who don't understand Aramaic. It's a struggle, but everybody gets the gist of what he is saying. Something dreadful is about to happen, and even if you didn't hear his words, it is written on his face. Andrew is speaking again: *'You are going to have the light just a little while longer,'* he translates. *'Walk while you have the light, before darkness overtakes you'* (John 12:35).

Jesus doesn't speak for long. He is clearly exhausted, and he leaves with some of his followers to get some sleep.

Afterwards, Andrew and Philip tell you their story and you take the opportunity to ask about the dead man from Bethany. They explain how a close friend of Jesus had been dead for three days, but when Jesus arrived he had been brought back to life. They do not seem to be the kind of people to invent a story like this, and as you quiz them it strikes you that they answer very openly. These men have nothing at all to hide.

'If Jesus has the authority to raise the dead, why doesn't everyone believe in him?' you ask.

Philip explains, 'The amazing thing is that some of the ruling council attended Lazarus' burial. They know full well that something supernatural has happened. Yet after Lazarus was raised at Bethany, they became more aggressive and determined to destroy Jesus.'

Andrew agrees. 'That's right. We are sure some of them do believe that Jesus is the Christ, but they are afraid to show their hand in case they lose their position on the ruling council.' Andrew looks at you. 'If you want to follow Jesus, you have to lose the fear of what other people can do to you.'

There is quietness after that. Not a lot more can be said. As you make to leave, you are surprised to see that Jesus himself has joined you. He speaks quietly and directly to you: *'When a man believes in me, he does not believe in me only, but in the one who sent me. When he looks at me, he sees the one who sent me'* (John 12:44–45). His words are at once sharp and yet full of love. They are poetic, but there is no question what he is driving at. He has left you with a choice to make. Don't worry; he does this to everyone.

PART THREE
Jerusalem

11
The death of Jesus

The law said that adultery was wrong, but laws cannot control human feelings, and even deeply religious people have those. So it was not surprising that during one of Jesus' visits to Jerusalem he was asked about his attitude to sexual sin. This time, the Pharisees and teachers of the law allowed themselves a little creativity in the way they posed the question. It was rather clever and very brutal (see John 8:1–11).

As Jesus was teaching in the little section of the temple courtyard the team had requisitioned for their work, an excited crowd interrupted him. At the front some men frog-marched a frightened woman towards him. One of the Pharisees spoke. There was little respect in his voice. *'Teacher, this woman was caught in the act of adultery. In the Law Moses commands us to stone such women. Now what do you say?'*

The teacher said nothing at all, but knelt on the ground, drawing with his finger in the dust on the pavement. He knew it was a set-up designed to embarrass him, He had always endorsed the law and could not fail to do so now, but they knew he would not let them harm the woman. Anything he said would discredit him in the eyes of his followers and give his enemies ammunition to destroy him. Suddenly, he stood up and said quietly, *'If any one of you is without sin, let him be the first to throw a stone at her.'*

As Jesus returned to his doodling on the ground, the Pharisees looked at each other, itching to make a clever reply to the teacher's answer. John says the older ones were the first to realize they had been beaten, for they left very quickly. The teacher said nothing more, absent-mindedly drawing in the dust on the ground as if he had forgotten they were there. Then even the younger ones had to admit they had lost the chance to prove themselves in theological debate, and they left the temple too.

Jesus stood up and approached the woman. Perhaps he put his hands on her shoulders. His voice was gentle. *'Woman, where are they? Has no-one condemned you?'*

Breathing deeply to hold back the tears she said, *'No-one, sir.'*

'Then neither do I condemn you,' he replied. *'Go now and leave your life of sin.'*

Is forgiveness cheap?

Whether Jesus is telling the paralysed man that his sins are forgiven, or reassuring the woman after her ordeal in the temple, you cannot help feeling that there is something almost casual about the way he forgives. It would be easy to slip into thinking that he will always forgive and never condemn, because forgiveness is easy. Nothing could be further from the truth.

I find using a credit card very easy. You just walk into a shop, get the stuff you want and take it to the counter. Then you give the assistant your card and sign a slip of paper. No worries! It is so easy it is addictive. You pop into another shop and repeat the intoxicating experience. Reality reasserts itself only a few weeks later, when the credit-card bill hits the doormat. Suddenly you realize what you knew all along: the stuff you bought was not free; it has to be paid for.

Likewise, forgiveness is not free. God's law has been broken, and that means a penalty has to be paid. Every time Jesus forgave someone's sin he was freely giving them something he had to pay for himself. For Jesus, the bill hit the doormat when he died on the cross. John the Baptist had anticipated this when he told his people that Jesus was '*the Lamb of God, who takes away the sin of the world*' (John 1:29). Jesus himself explained this concept carefully in his last meeting with his own disciples before he died. It was essential that they should understand the real significance of what was about to happen.

The Last Supper

That last meeting was a Passover celebration with his disciples in an upstairs room they had borrowed for the occasion. The mood was sombre; he was beginning to say some strange things about his imminent death. The Passover was a ritual meal, with each course designed to trigger memories of Israel's liberation from slavery in Egypt. Jesus and his friends were remembering the birth of their nation and seeing themselves once more as privileged members of a community rescued from slavery and brought into a special relationship with God.

If you had been there, you would not only be

remembering a distant historical event. Passover was part of your self-understanding, designed to bring you back to your roots and to help you see yourself as part of what God was doing on the stage of world history. You would have gone through this ritual with your family every year since your birth. Its words and movements would have been as familiar to you then as a Christmas nativity play is to a primary-school teacher today.

The meal includes unleavened bread (made without yeast). You know exactly what will be done and said. You would expect Jesus to take this bread and say: 'Blessed art thou, O Lord our God, King of the universe, who brings forth bread from the earth' – which is exactly what he did say. You know he will go on to explain its significance, because that's what the head of the table always does. You know the words by heart: 'This is the bread of affliction, the poor bread which our fathers ate in the land of Egypt. Let all who are hungry come and eat. Let all who are in need share in the hope of the Passover.'

This is what you are expecting as Jesus takes the bread. But when he lifts it up for everyone to see, his words leave the group stunned: *'This is my body given for you; do this in remembrance of me'* (Luke 22:19). His body? In remembrance of *him*, not of the rescue from Egypt? It is a shocking moment. An ancient ritual has been set aside and Jesus has put himself in its place.

The night before his execution, Jesus used the Passover to explain that his death had a spiritual significance beyond the disciples' wildest dreams. A new liberation was about to take place, and Jesus would pay for it with his life.

The downfall of Jesus

In the early days, Jesus had aroused suspicion but was perfectly free to get on with what he wanted to do. The establishment may have disapproved, but they hadn't seen him as especially dangerous. This attitude of tolerance had changed quickly. They had insisted that he should not heal on a Sabbath, the Jewish holy day. But Jesus refused to allow ritual considerations to prevent his showing mercy to those in need.

It was Jesus' repeated claims about himself that got him into deeper and deeper trouble. The first Christian believers soon decided that his words amounted to a claim to deity, and the Pharisees had reached the same conclusion. For them, no sign or miracle was impressive enough; Jesus was a blasphemer and had to pay the ultimate price. On top of this, the diverse cliques and interest groups in Jerusalem rapidly concluded that Jesus was of no use to them. The Zealots wouldn't back him because he didn't advocate violence. His family was poor, so the Sadducees thought he was a joke. He had given the Pharisees such a hard time that they wanted his blood. By Passover time in the third year of his public life, these factions were surprisingly unanimous about Jesus. *'Crucify him!'* was their verdict. Only the ordinary 'people of the land' remained loyal, and they didn't count.

Yet Jesus' continuing popularity with a large number of people did create a problem for the establishment. Crowds always surrounded him, and it was hard for the Pharisees to see how they could arrest him without a fuss. A wrong move at this point could cause a riot, and that would demonstrate their incompetence to the Romans. Timing was critical if they were to snatch Jesus without souring relations with the representatives of Rome.

It was not only the Pharisees who had a problem with Jesus; there were opponents among his own supporters, too. Judas Iscariot had already argued about the uses to which the team's money was put, and some of the disciples suspected that he helped himself to the funds from time to time. Whatever his motives, Judas switched sides and initiated a discussion with the Pharisees about ways of arresting Jesus quietly (Matthew 26:14–16). For Jesus' enemies, this was a gift. Judas knew his movements intimately and could lead their people to him when there were few supporters present.

On the way out of the city by night, Jesus and his team were jumped on by the high priest's personal guard. In the darkness, Judas led the guards to Jesus. Peter had a swipe at one of the aggressors with a sword, but Jesus stopped him. It was over in seconds, and the disciples were left leaderless. Only Peter found the courage to follow the swat team to the high priest's house, but even his courage soon failed him and he left. Jesus was alone.

Shopping for a verdict

He was taken to the Sanhedrin, or ruling council, for a preliminary hearing. There were laws about how such a trial should be conducted and, in their haste to get a quick result, many of them were broken. The high priest, Caiaphas, conducted it personally, at one point ordering, *'Tell us if you are the Christ, the Son of God.'* Jesus said he was, and the priest hit the roof. *'He has spoken blasphemy! Why do we need any more witnesses?'* The council agreed that he was worthy of death (Matthew 26:63–66).

Here they were faced with a problem. It seems that the Sanhedrin did not at this time have authority to execute anyone, though they may have been given it at a later date.

They had to involve the Romans and persuade them that Jesus should be killed. The trial of Jesus moved to the chambers of the governor, Pontius Pilate. But the Roman was in no mood to execute a perfect stranger on the say-so of the fastidious Sanhedrin, who wouldn't even enter his house in case they became ceremonially unclean. Pilate had to meet with them outside. You can imagine that he was not inclined to grant them any favours.

Luke's Gospel describes the way the Sanhedrin tried to wheedle Pilate into executing Jesus. 'He subverts the nation, opposes paying taxes to Caesar and says he is a king,' they said (Luke 23:1–2). But Pilate was in an awkward mood, and when he realized that Jesus was a Galilean he saw his way out. Anything from Galilee was Herod's business and, as the tetrarch was in Jerusalem, the Sanhedrin was packed off to his palace to try to get a result.

To Pilate's huge delight, the Sanhedrin got no joy there either. In the musical *Jesus Christ Superstar*, Herod is presented as a bored playboy who languidly uses Jesus for his amusement before sending the Sanhedrin packing. This is certainly the impression you get from Luke's account of this event. Once more they have to return to Pilate. But now relationships had soured, and the ruling council was prepared to get nasty with the Roman governor. The word went out to their supporters to gather outside Pilate's house; the stakes were being raised.

Perhaps Pilate found something in Jesus that he wanted to defend, or maybe he was so heartily sick of the antics of the Sanhedrin that he would have done anything to frustrate them. He may have been intimidated by a message from his wife, telling him of a frightening dream she'd had about Jesus (Matthew 27:19). For whatever reason, Luke describes Pilate urging the Sanhedrin to let him off with a lighter punishment than death. His verdict is so remarkable it is worth quoting in full: *'I have examined him in your presence and found no basis for your charges against him. Neither has Herod, for he sent him back to us; as you can see, he has done nothing to deserve death. Therefore I will punish him and then release him'* (Luke 23:13–16). Jesus had been tried by a biased court, without defence and with the testimony of carefully selected witnesses. Despite this, he had been declared innocent by two authorities, and the governor was offering the council a reasonable way out.

The Sanhedrin could not let Jesus get off, and they began to incite the crowd that was now gathering outside Pilate's house to bay for the rabbi's blood. This new pressure changed the situation, and Pilate sensed that he was losing control. Rome would question his competence if a riot ensued as a result of his obstinate refusal to execute a Galilean labourer. Power was passing from the governor into the hands of the mob. Jesus' fate was in the hands of a crowd that had been pulled together with the purpose of pressurizing the governor into thinking an insurrection was about to happen. He had no chance.

Pilate had developed the custom of releasing a condemned prisoner at Passover time. A man called Barabbas was waiting to be executed, and Pilate offered the people a choice: Jesus or Barabbas. It was no contest. 'Give us Barabbas!' they yelled.

Death on a cross

I once met a woman who had been a nurse in a refugee camp in Cambodia at the height of the war with the Khmer Rouge. She had been forced to watch as a young Cambodian was taken out and nailed by his hands and feet to a tree. He was left there to die. She never recovered from the experience, and the memory scars her life to this day. Such was the impact of a crucifixion.

The Romans took 'cruel and unusual punishment' seriously and used it as a weapon to intimidate the masses. Over two hundred years they had perfected the art of making a man's death as humiliating and as long-drawn-out as possible. Pilate now committed Jesus into the hands of his execution artists. First there was a flogging. Many victims died at this point, before the ritual could go further. Then there was a grisly public procession as the victim carried his own cross (or part of it) through the city to the place of execution. There he was fastened to the cross, his arms spread-eagled and his feet skewered to the wood with a single nail. The cross was hoisted up to stand upright.

Though the victim may have been less than a metre off the ground, his death was slow and excruciating. Hanging like this, he could not breathe, so he had to push his weight on to the nail to raise himself to get a breath. Sometimes a small wooden beam was nailed on the cross as a seat; it relieved the pain, but made the torture last longer. Men could take several days to die of asphyxiation, hunger and shock. The entire process was public, and people were encouraged to come and make fun of the helpless victims as they hung there. This was crowd control Roman-style.

Jesus took the beating and the ridicule that followed. The soldiers dressed him up as a king and pushed a laurel crown down on to his head, only this one was made from sharp thorns, not laurels. He didn't manage to carry his cross all the way through the city, and a man called Simon was press-ganged by the soldiers into carrying it for him. Outside the city, a moment before Jesus' cross was raised,

Pilate got his final dig at the Sanhedrin. A soldier nailed a plaque over Jesus' head: *'Jesus of Nazareth, the King of the Jews'*, it said (John 19:19). He had written it in three languages so that everyone got the message. The Jewish chief priests were furious and demanded to have it removed. 'Like it or lump it!' was the gist of Pilate's reply.

It was a ghastly business, yet the Gospel writers say little about the physical suffering of Jesus. Most of the detailed description of crucifixion you have just read is reduced to one phrase in the Gospels: ' ... *there they crucified him*' (Luke 23:33). Guided by Jesus' teaching about the Passover, their interest lay in the spiritual significance of what was happening. Seven times Jesus gets enough breath to gasp a short sentence from the cross. This victim of death by torture prays for his oppressors: *'Father, forgive them, for they do not know what they are doing'* (Luke 23:34). He cries in desolation, *'My God, my God, why have you forsaken me?'* (Mark 15:34). As his death approaches, the sky darkens and a supernatural blackness settles over Jerusalem. Then Jesus said, *'It is finished!'* (John 19:30). Before the echo of the words had faded, he was dead.

What did his executioners fail to understand about what they were doing? Why was God's Son abandoned by his Father? What was finished?

The meaning of the cross

You cannot read the Gospels' account of the trial and execution of Jesus without an uneasy feeling that something is missing. Here is a man who lived such a vigorous and purposeful life, always taking the initiative, responding to questions, refusing to let powerful enemies get away with anything. Yet from the moment of his arrest he becomes passive. Jesus hardly speaks a word as he is frog-marched around by the people trying to engineer his death. Where is his power? What has happened to his ability to persuade? He was so effective in exposing religious nonsense before; why can't he turn his fire on the legal nonsense being perpetrated at his trial?

Jesus was not terrified into submission, for he still defied Pilate, and did not hesitate to confirm his claim to be the Son of God. That leaves us with only one possibility: Jesus the powerful chose to become powerless; the persuader chose to be silent.

The point was not lost on those who turned out to sneer at him as he hung dying on the cross. '*He trusts in God. Let God rescue him now if he wants him, for he said, "I am the Son of God"*' (Matthew 27:43).

Simon Peter remembered this moment vividly. This is how he describes it:

> *When they hurled their insults at him, he did not retaliate; when he suffered, he made no threats. Instead, he entrusted himself to him who judges justly. He himself bore our sins in his body on the tree, so that we might die to sins and live for righteousness; by his wounds you have been healed. For you were like sheep going astray, but now you have returned to the Shepherd and Overseer of your souls* (1 Peter 2:23–25).

Jesus deliberately sacrificed his life, and this became the route by which people could recover their lost relationship with God. His death works in the same way that the first Passover worked for the nation of Israel; a bloody death averts God's judgment, which destroys the power that held us captive, and our new life as God's people begins (see Exodus 12:1–30; 1 Corinthians 5:7). That's why the

Gospel writers were not at all embarrassed to present Jesus as the divine Son of Man and Son of God who nevertheless dies in desolation on the cross. On that cross the bill for forgiveness hit the doormat. God's anger against our sin was poured down on Jesus like a mighty waterfall, and it crushed him: *'My God, my God, why have you forsaken me?'* He chose to take the curse and to be a sacrifice to liberate his people into a new life.

This is why Jesus introduced his disciples to the spiritual significance of his death at the Last Supper. He is the new Passover, only this time we are being liberated not from slavery to the Egyptians, but from the power of sin to destroy our lives. Jesus' last words, *'It is finished'*, now take on a new meaning. His life had reached its climax in his sacrificial death; the work he came to do was over. *It* was finished, but *he* was not! The story of Jesus does not end here.

12

The resurgence of the Jesus movement

If it had been up to the Sanhedrin, Jesus' body would have hung on the cross until it decayed. That was certainly the way the Romans maximized the crowd-controlling potential of crucifixion, but there were influential Jews who were not prepared to let that happen.

Two years before, a member of the Sanhedrin had been investigating Jesus. They met and talked together long into the night. (You can read an account of their rather technical conversation in John 3:1–21.) The man's name was Nicodemus, and he must have been impressed, because later he defended Jesus at a meeting of the Sanhedrin. We don't know where he was when his colleagues were engineering the crucifixion, but when he heard about their plans he decided to do something very bold to express his opposition to the execution. He got together with. Joseph of Arimathea, another aristocratic Jew who had secretly believed Jesus' teaching about the kingdom. (There must have been others whose names we do not know.) Joseph had asked Pilate for permission to take Jesus' body and give it a decent burial. Nicodemus brought along a lavish quantity of herbal preparations to embalm it.

When the two men reached Golgotha Hill, just outside the city, they found that Jesus was already dead. One of the soldiers had stuck a spear into his chest cavity to make sure. His was an unsentimental professional and he knew his trade well. He didn't want to cut down a hospital case; he wanted a corpse (John 19:31–42).

The twilight of the Jesus movement

All that now remained of Jesus' team were the women whose support had sustained the work for the last three years. They stood at a distance and watched as he was taken down from the cross (Luke 23:49, 55). The men had run away; as prime targets of a further purge by the Sanhedrin they were in great danger. It was simply not safe for them to be seen out in the open.

As the women watched the body being taken from the cross, they could not have known that it was in good hands. Joseph was wealthy enough to have a carefully prepared family tomb nearby, and he supervised the burial of Jesus in his own grave. This tomb would have resembled a small cave, cut into solid rock and closed up with an immense circular stone. After Jesus' embalmed body was placed on a shelf inside, the stone would have been rolled over the entrance to seal the tomb. Joseph and Nicodemus had to act quickly, for the Sabbath was about to begin and no kind of work could take place once it had started.

So ended the Jesus movement. With the disciples dispersed and only a few women left to visit the tomb after the Sabbath, all the high hopes of those three years of power and glory were dashed. Pilate could forget about Jesus; he had a career to pursue. The Sanhedrin could enjoy a peaceful Sabbath for a change, untroubled by disturbing stories of illegal healings. Jesus' friends would return to their native Galilee, and go back to their old business life.

As you know, however, that is not quite what happened.

About two months later ...

Peter and John were on their way to the temple in Jerusalem when they noticed a disabled man begging from the people going in to worship. Peter stopped, and in a few seconds the beggar was miraculously healed. Chaos ensued, and the two disciples were quickly arrested and taken off the streets. Soon, they were solemnly brought before the Sanhedrin. They were in deep trouble, as their captors were not prepared to tolerate a resurgence of the Jesus movement. But this time the team did not back down. It was Peter who spoke:

> *Rulers and elders of the people! If we are being called*
> *to account today for an act of kindness shown to a*
> *cripple and are asked how he was healed, then know*
> *this, you and all the people of Israel: It is by the name*
> *of Jesus Christ of Nazareth, whom you crucified but*
> *whom God raised from the dead, that this man stands*
> *before you healed. He is*
>
> > *'the stone you builders rejected,*
> > *which has become the capstone.'*

*Salvation is found in no-one else, for there is no
other name under heaven given to men by whom we
must be saved* (Acts 4:8–12).

If the ruling council was not going to tolerate heresy,
neither were the disciples in any mood to be intimidated
by them. Within a few weeks of Jesus' death, they were
confronting his enemies with their responsibility for it,
and telling them that their whole religious system was now
redundant because something new had arrived to replace
it. They were putting their heads into the lion's mouth.
What could possibly explain this turnaround in the
confidence of the disciples, and the vigorous rise of the
Christian movement that was to follow?

Peter was in no doubt. There had been a new development in the Jesus story. He had risen from the dead.

A fly on the wall with John

There is no better way to get a flavour of what had
happened in the weeks before this confrontation than to
see it through the eyes of someone who saw most of what
happened himself. John claims to be such a person and
begins his description with what happened to Mary
Magdalene.

*Early on the first day of the week, while it was still
dark, Mary Magdalene went to the tomb and saw that
the stone had been removed from the entrance. So she
came running to Simon Peter and the other disciple,
the one Jesus loved, and said, 'They have taken the
Lord out of the tomb, and we don't know where they
have put him!'* (John 20:1–2).

As far as Mary was concerned, the authorities must have removed the body of Jesus. She seems genuinely closed to the possibility that anything else might have happened. So were the disciples who returned to the tomb with her. John tells us that he was there (he is 'the disciple Jesus loved'), and his description of what happened is bristling with the kind of detail that would stick in the mind of an eye-witness:

Peter and the other disciple started for the tomb. Both were running, but the other disciple outran Peter and reached the tomb first. He bent over and looked in at the strips of linen lying there but did not go in. Then Simon Peter, who was behind him, arrived and went into the tomb. He saw the strips of linen lying there, as well as the burial cloth that had been around Jesus' head. The cloth was folded up by itself, separate from the linen. Finally the other disciple, who had reached the tomb first, also went inside (John 20:3–8).

There is such a vividness in John's description, with so many details jostling in his head at once. The race to the grave, who got there first, the details about the cloths, who went in first: it isn't the kind of thing you make up, is it? Puzzled, Peter and John return to the city, leaving Mary weeping softly outside the cave.

Shortly after, Mary returned to the city and found the others. She brought with her an incredible story. As she looked once more into the tomb, she saw two figures sitting where Jesus had been. They told her that he had risen from the dead. Then, she said, Jesus himself had spoken to her! He really was alive!

It is not hard to imagine the sceptical reaction she got.

Luke says they thought she had gone mad, and we probably would have done so too.

That is the most plausible explanation, surely. As she sat on her own in the early morning, emotionally raw and very tired, it must have been some kind of vision. Mary's longing to see Jesus again had expressed itself as an all-too-real dream. She was not mad as such, but she could hardly expect people to believe her story.

John goes on to tell us how the disciples were shaken out of this illusion:

> *On the evening of that first day of the week, when the disciples were together, with the doors locked for fear of the Jews, Jesus came and stood among them and said, 'Peace be with you!' After he said this, he showed them his hands and side. The disciples were overjoyed when they saw the Lord* (John 20:19–20).

This was the first of many collective experiences of Jesus' resurrection. Soon a great many people would be able to tell of their own meeting with him; some were in large groups and others in twos and threes. All were adamant that the person they saw was Jesus himself. But there is something odd about their descriptions of Jesus at this stage. He often just appears from nowhere, and leaves them the same way. Was this the real Jesus, or some kind of spirit that clung to the disciples, a ghost of their friend?

Perhaps this was Thomas's interpretation of what had happened. He was not present when Jesus had appeared to the others, and could not believe that his friend had risen from the dead. John quotes him as saying, *'Unless I see the nail marks in his hands and put my finger where the nails were, and put my hand into his side, I will not believe it.'*

(John 20:25). He wanted something more tangible than a man who seemed to walk through walls.

John tells us what happened next:

A week later his disciples were in the house again, and Thomas was with them. Though the doors were locked, Jesus came and stood among them and said, 'Peace be with you!' Then he said to Thomas, 'Put your finger here; see my hands. Reach out your hand and put it into my side. Stop doubting and believe.'

Thomas said to him, 'My Lord and my God!'

Then Jesus told him, 'Because you have seen me, you have believed; blessed are those who have not seen and yet have believed' (John 20:26–29).

The Gospels make it clear that Jesus was not a semi-transparent or insubstantial, ghostly figure after his resurrection. Thomas could handle Jesus' body, and Luke tells of him eating a piece of fish to convince his friends that he was not a ghost (Luke 24:37–43). The authentic voice of the earliest followers of Jesus says he had physically risen from the dead.

Poetry and perjury

A lot of people find it hard to believe in a physical resurrection. Some prefer the thought that the disciples used the metaphor of resurrection to convey their real point, which was that, though Jesus was gone for ever, his ideas would live on. They see John's vivid description as a literary device and little more. The problem here is that the Gospels' descriptions do not read like an extended metaphor. They tell us passionately about a staggering event that really happened. Peter was not afraid to declare the unthinkable reality of a physical resurrection to a court that could have killed him. Why is it that some twenty-first-century Christians are afraid to affirm the same thing? What are they frightened of?

Some rightly point out that there are apparent inconsistencies in the Gospel accounts. For example, each Gospel writer has a slightly different combination of women going to visit the tomb when the Sabbath is over. But this is no reason to jump to the conclusion that the resurrection accounts are garbled or just invented. In fact, it is the very roughness of the different testimonies that gives them authenticity. Stories that tie up too tightly lead real investigators to suspect dishonest collusion.

In 1990 two wealthy young Englishmen, Darius Guppy and Benedict Marsh, were robbed at gunpoint in their hotel room in New York. They were diamond merchants, and claimed that the thief had taken gems worth £1.8 million. The New York Police Department set up an investigation, but from the beginning the detectives suspected that the two Old Etonians had set the whole thing up. What made them suspicious was the fact that both of them answered the detectives in the same way. There were no inconsistencies in their story; every detail tied up. But the NYPD couldn't prove anything at the time.

Two years later, an American was arrested for armed robbery in London, and confessed to having staged the New York job. Both the jewels and the robbery were a fake, and Lloyds of London had been defrauded of £1.8 million. The detectives' suspicions turned out to be justified.

The apparent inconsistencies in the resurrection accounts actually serve to illustrate the integrity of the writers. The early church made no attempt to smooth the wrinkles out. A dead man had come back to life, and his friends' memories of the event reflect the excitement and delirium they must have felt at the time. If they had all said the same thing in the same sequence in the same words, we would be right to be suspicious. The resurrection testimonies are not perjury, and they are not mere poetry; they tell us with integrity that a man has risen from death.

Saul of Tarsus

For all the evidence in favour of the resurrection of Jesus, there were many who could not bring themselves to believe it. Naturally, the Pharisees were keen to suppress any information that would encourage the Jesus movement, and this led to out-and-out persecution within a very short time. Saul of Tarsus, the man with the thoroughbred Jewish pedigree whom we met in chapter 6, began to round up believers enthusiastically and to organize their imprisonment and execution. He helped to preside over the death of the first Christian martyr, a man called Stephen.

Saul was on his way to Syria to root out more Christians when he had an experience that changed his life (Acts 9:1–30). In a letter to a Christian community in Corinth he adds his experience to the testimony of the A team:

For what I received I passed on to you as of first importance: that Christ died for our sins according to the Scriptures, that he was buried, that he was raised on the third day according to the Scriptures, and that he appeared to Peter, and then to the Twelve. After that, he appeared to more than five hundred of the

> brothers at the same time, most of whom are still
> living, though some have fallen asleep. Then he ap-
> peared to James, then to all the apostles, and last of all
> he appeared to me also, as to one abnormally born.
>
> For I am the least of the apostles and do not even
> deserve to be called an apostle, because I persecuted the
> church of God (1 Corinthians 15:3–9).

This meeting shattered Saul. From that moment, this
highly trained Jewish scholar (also known as Paul) became
Jesus' ambassador to the non-Jewish world. The man who
thought the resurrection was a complete fabrication
became the one who communicated its message more
effectively than any of Jesus' original team. Jesus really was
still in business!

Confrontation in the temple

The power of the risen Jesus was the only explanation
Peter offered the Sanhedrin in the temple the day he was
arrested for healing the beggar. The man who had once
run away in terror was now confronting the people who
had pressurized Pilate into ordering Jesus' crucifixion. His
courage came from the fact that he was convinced that
Jesus really was alive; not a ghost, a dream or even a
religious metaphor. No-one would run such risks for
anything as insubstantial as a literary device. The only
explanation that fits the facts is the simplest one. Jesus had
indeed risen from the dead.

According to Luke, Jesus had continued to appear to
his disciples over a period of forty days. He says they were
given 'many convincing proofs' that he was alive (Acts
1:3). They were going to need this conviction, because the
apostles would soon be taking on the world in the same

way that Jesus had taken on Jerusalem. Before long, some of them would pay the price for not cowering before the Sanhedrin. They were so convinced the resurrection was a reality that they were fearless in the face of their own deaths.

Waiting for the Spirit

During this forty-day seminar Jesus continued to teach them about the kingdom of God. Teachings they could never have understood before his death and resurrection now became clear to the apostles. This message was to be passed on to others in the Jesus movement, whose job it was to treasure it and spread it around the world. The New Testament that we have today is full of detailed explanation of the events in Jesus' life, flowing from the knowledge that was given to the apostles at this time.

Towards the end of this period, Jesus gathered his disciples together and briefed them for the last time:

> *Do not leave Jerusalem, but wait for the gift my Father promised, which you have heard me speak about. For John baptised with water, but in a few days you will be baptised with the Holy Spirit ... and you will be my witnesses in Jerusalem, and in all Judea and Samaria, and to the ends of the earth* (Acts 1:4–8).

Then he left them, physically ascending into heaven before their eyes. Once more the disciples found themselves alone, but this time they knew that the Jesus movement had only just begun. They also knew that their master would return one day, though they had no idea when this would be. For the moment their job was to wait for the gift Jesus had promised. He had insisted that the team wait in Jerusalem until the Holy Spirit fell on them.

It was not long before the promise was fulfilled. The Holy Spirit came on the Jewish feast-day called Pentecost. It was now that the A team hit the streets to tell the crowds in Jerusalem about the death and resurrection of Jesus. Within a few hours, the Jesus movement had three thousand new disciples to look after. It was not a flash in the pan; their radical boldness continued into the days that followed. Even when the twelve were hauled before the ruling council, there was no stopping them. Peter and John defied the Sanhedrin and, when they were solemnly told not to spread the message about Jesus, they refused. As soon as they left the building, Peter and his friends picked up where they had left off. Jesus was back in business and was going multinational.

The rest is history.

13

Following Jesus in the twenty-first century

My first job after leaving college was to be warden of a seaside nature reserve in Wales. It was a beautiful place, with low, bracken-covered hills sweeping down to the beach. That first summer, it was crowded every day with families on holiday. We were in the middle of a long drought and the weather was glorious. Children made dens in the long ferns while their parents sunbathed on the beach nearby.

One day, someone ran into my office. 'There's a fire in the bracken and it's spreading fast!'

I ran to see, and was appalled by what was happening. The previous year's growth of bracken, which had died back and was now bone dry, had caught fire. The wind was strong and the fire was spreading rapidly, heading straight for the beach and the children in the under-growth. I ran to the top of a sand dune. Looking down, I could see dozens of kids in danger of being suddenly enveloped by the fire. The only hope was to alert the adults on the beach, so I ran down the dune as fast as I could to warn them.

I still feel amazed at what happened next. Instead of going to find their children, the families on the beach just laughed. They could see the flames and smell the smoke, but they assumed that I was exaggerating the problem and that their kids would be fine. I was angry. They just did not appreciate how fast and furious the fire was.

Looking back, I think I can understand their problem. We both knew there was a fire, and could see the smoke. The difference was that I had experienced the fire, whereas they had only seen it at a distance.

I feel the same way as I reach the end of this book. Jesus is not a distant historical figure, but a living presence in my everyday life. He's not just a fascinating religious teacher, but the baseline for everything I am or seek to be. Let me tell you as clearly as I can: I have felt the fire, and I want you to experience it too!

You may be one of those people who sense that God is out there somewhere, but he is remote and mysterious. You feel a need to know him better, but it is hard to see how you can. That sense of separation is real and has become part of the human condition. This gulf is the effect of sin – our refusal to allow God to take his rightful place as Lord of our lives. Breaking the law of God like this involves a penalty. We need to be forgiven if we want to cross the gulf, but the cost of forgiveness is a price we can't pay. The Son of God became a carpenter in Nazareth to bridge this gulf. Here's a reminder of how he did that.

He came from heaven to earth

Jesus' words and works led people gradually to conclude that he was more than a religious teacher; he was God incarnate. His friends and his enemies grew to understand that he was claiming to be no less, and could back up that claim with his actions. That gives us a huge clue to the meaning of the mysterious word 'God'. Left to our imaginations, we have to load the word 'God' with some kind of meaning for ourselves. If Jesus is God in human form, we have some help. He is our starting-point for understanding what God is like. Jesus once said, *'Anyone who has seen me has seen the Father'* (John 14:9). Jesus bridges the gulf by making the mysterious creator of the universe understandable to ordinary people. He is God in a form that we can comprehend.

He went to a death on a cross

Jesus made it clear that his life was a rescue mission. He put it like this: *'The Son of Man did not come to be served, but to serve, and to give his life as a ransom for many'* (Matthew 20:28). His death was a *ransom* payment, as if we were prisoners of a terrorist gang that demanded the payment of a ransom before we could be set free. Jesus died in our place, liberating us from the power of sin and the punishment it deserves. Jesus bridges the gulf by liberating us from sin on the cross.

He went from the cross to the grave

At the end of Jesus' trial, Barabbas went free and Jesus was sent out to die. The cross Jesus was skewered to was possibly the very beam of wood earmarked for the notorious prisoner. Jesus died instead of Barabbas. The first Christians often talked of how Jesus had died as a substitute for us. It was as though, in dying, he had absorbed God's righteous anger against our sin. His friend

Peter put it like this: *'Christ died for sins ... the righteous for the unrighteous, to bring you to God'* (1 Peter 3:18). Jesus bridges the gulf by enduring God's justice in our place.

He physically rose from the dead

If the cross had been the end of the story, the Jesus movement would have been dead in the water. Paul, who was so profoundly changed by his meeting with the risen Jesus, once wrote that Jesus was triumphantly declared to be the Son of God by his resurrection from the dead (Romans 1:4). But why didn't Jesus stay on earth? What was the ascension back to heaven about?

Jesus himself explained that he was going to leave his friends so that the Holy Spirit could be sent to them. So today, instead of having to go to Galilee to see Jesus, his actual presence is felt in the lives of those who put their faith in him. He is no longer limited by geography; the Holy Spirit makes the presence of Jesus real wherever his people are. Jesus bridges the gulf by sending the Holy Spirit, so that we can know friendship with him personally and intimately.

Becoming a disciple

When Jesus challenged his first followers, he said, *'The time has come ... The kingdom of God is near. Repent and believe the good news!'* (Mark 1:15).

Most people cherish their right to run their own lives and to make up their own rules as they go along. Turning away from this attitude and allowing Jesus to be Lord of our lives is called *repentance*. It means seeing the bankruptcy of our own ideas and the richness of his, and responding to Jesus as our king. Of course, this means that we need to trust him, to respond to his claim to be the Son of God with personal faith. We must *believe*. We have seen that God's kingly rule broke into people's lives when they put their trust in Jesus. The same is true today. Jesus' twenty-first-century friends are people who have made this decision and have found that living under his lordship is a lifestyle that works.

By the way, don't be put off by the word 'disciple'. It is from a Latin word that means 'learner'. A disciple is not an elite Christian, but someone who is following Jesus and trying to learn from him how to live a life that is filled with the presence of God.

My using a phrase like 'feeling the fire' may lead you to think that a stratospheric spiritual experience is essential before you step out in faith. A lot of people are stalled in their spiritual search because they think they have to wait for an ecstatic experience. But different people feel God's presence in different ways, and our feelings are unreliable guides to making life-changing decisions. An emotional experience of God tends to follow on from giving our lives to him in repentance and faith. Some will feel a great high; others will not. What matters is making the right response to the Son of God, who loved you and gave himself for you. Everyone who knows about Jesus has a choice to make, and now that choice is yours.

Where do I go from here?

Understanding who Jesus is and what he has done brings each of us to a point of decision. He has built the bridge, and we can cross it if we choose to trust him and to live his way. That is the decision each of us must make. Where you go from here will depend on the stage you have reached in your own spiritual journey. It would make sense to reflect on this before you go any further. Perhaps one of the headings below sums up your present position.

No questions. Where do I sign?

Do you remember that copy of Luke's Gospel I was given in Geneva? All that summer I worked my way through it as we climbed the stunning peaks of the Mont Blanc range. Gradually, this distant God became real to me as I grew to know Jesus. Later that year I was reading Matthew when I stumbled across the Beatitudes. In those short proverbs I found a definition of what I would like to become. Jesus had grown on me, and I wanted to follow him. Is that where you are at?

It is unlikely that you have no questions at all. But you know enough to say that you too are ready to launch out as a disciple of Christ. If so, you need to talk to him. That is, speak to him as a living person, and explain that you want to give your life to him. It can be a little difficult to do this if you are not used to speaking to God, so at the end of this chapter I have suggested a short prayer that you could use to do this. Remember that you cannot be a Christian on your own. (I know, I tried it for about six months!) You need to find a church where you will be supported in you your new life. If you have problems with this and live in the UK, e-mail me at ChezBurke@aol.com and I will help you out.

Very drawn to Jesus, but not ready to commit myself

You will never reach the point where all your questions have been answered, but you do need to get to the point where you feel you are not just leaping into the dark.

Remember, Jesus compared you to the merchant looking for fine pearls. You are on a treasure hunt, so you need to give it some time and thought. Why not get hold of one of the Gospels (I think either John or Luke is best for this) and read it through over a few weeks, a chapter each day? This will give you a full picture of the person we are talking about. You may like to start each day's read with a prayer like this: 'God, I don't know if you are there or not, but if you are, I want to know for myself. Help me to understand as I read, and if you speak to me I will listen.'

Jesus promised that if we seek him sincerely, we will find him. Be careful, though: I know dozens of people whose lives have been changed by doing this. Get ready to be like the merchant in Jesus' story: when you know you have found what you were looking for, put everything on the line to enter the kingdom.

Full of questions; where are the answers?

I know how you feel. Speaking personally, I have been a Christian for almost twenty-five years and I still find the Christian faith satisfying to the mind and emotions; it feels good and *thinks* good, too. But I am still bothered by some bits of Christian teaching I don't understand. If you want to chase up some outstanding issues, you may find the booklist at the end helpful. But beware of two pitfalls. First, some of the questions we ask have no known answer (such as 'Where did God come from?' or 'Why is country and western music so popular?'), so be realistic in your search for answers. Secondly, are you sure that your questions are genuine? Or are you just creating a pseudo-intellectual smokescreen to stop God from getting through to you? I am sorry if that last point hurt, but it is a question worth asking.

I want to, but I can't

The challenge to follow Jesus is scary, and a lot of people hold back for fear that they will fail. No-one wants to make a commitment to Jesus and then find they are unable to keep it up. If this is how you feel, you are special! You have discovered something that over-confident people tend to miss: the Christian life is impossible, and there is no way you can live it successfully under your own steam. Unlike many others, you have a realistic assessment of the situation, and it is you that Jesus had in mind when he said, *'Blessed are the poor in spirit, for theirs is the kingdom of heaven'* (Matthew 5:3). That feeling of unworthiness is the ideal launchpad into real discipleship.

This is why Jesus sent the Holy Spirit to work in us. He does not ask us to go solo; his Spirit gives us the resources we need to live a new life. That does not mean that we never fail, but it does mean that we are never alone. As we have seen, Jesus' original disciples were very ordinary people; they were not elite troops. Just as he was patient with their many failures, so he will be patient with us. If you feel unworthy – you are ready!

Taking the plunge

If you are ready to cross the bridge, you must take a step, trusting that the bridge will hold your weight and get you to the other side safely. Don't be afraid; it has held the weight of many who have crossed before you, and it will hold yours too.

Starting out with Jesus is the beginning of a friendship, and like all relationships it begins when we talk. If you are not sure what to say to him, try something like this:

Lord Jesus Christ,

like your first followers, I have come to realize that you are the Son of God.

I believe that you came to earth to show me the way to God.

I know that you died on the cross to pay the price of my sin.

I believe that you rose from the dead and that you give new life.

I turn away from my sin and put my trust in you for the future.

Please give me the gift of your Holy Spirit, because I want to live for you.

Thank you, Lord Jesus.

Amen.

Where to find out more

30 Days, by Nicky Gumbel (HTB Publications, 1999). A great way to begin reading the Bible regularly and relating it to your life. Gives you a passage to read each day for a month and a useful explanation of it.

The Jesus I Never Knew, by Philip Yancey (Marshall Pickering, 1995). A fuller exploration of the life of Jesus by an outstanding American writer. This is the book I wish I had written! If you are serious about finding out more, this is the best book to go for.

Jesus, Life or Legend? by Carsten Peter Thiede (Lion, 1990). The story of how the Gospels were written. Told by an expert 'scroll detective', but in a popular style.

The Message of Luke, by Michael Wilcock (IVP, 1979). A more detailed guide to the best Gospel to start with if you want to begin studying the source material behind this book.

Searching Issues, by Nicky Gumbel (Kingsway, 1994). If you are saying, 'Yes, but what about suffering ...

science ... sexuality ...' and so on, this book is for you.

The Fight, by John White (IVP, 1977). If you are looking for an introduction to living as a Christian, this is a classic you must read.